# BE OPPORTUNITY-MINDED

# BE OPPORTUNITY MINDED

## START GROWING YOUR CAREER NOW

### CAITLIN WILLIAMS

ALA Editions

CHICAGO 2019

**Caitlin Williams**, PhD, is an author, speaker, and professional development consultant. She has spent the last thirty years working in the field of career development through writing, speaking, coaching, and teaching. Caitlin has had the honor of conducting career coaching for ALA attendees at its twice-yearly conferences since 2000. She has also presented and contributed numerous articles and podcasts to ALA. She has written two previous books on career and workplace topics (one title has been translated into Korean). Caitlin is retired from teaching at San Jose State University, and she is looking forward to new adventures and opportunities!

© 2019 by the American Library Association

Extensive effort has gone into ensuring the reliability of the information in this book; however, the publisher makes no warranty, express or implied, with respect to the material contained herein.

ISBN: 978-0-8389-1772-5 (paper)

**Library of Congress Cataloging-in-Publication Data**
Names: Williams, Caitlin, 1949– author.
Title: Be opportunity-minded : start growing your career now / Caitlin
   Williams.
Description: Chicago : ALA Editions, 2019. | Includes bibliographical
   references and index.
Identifiers: LCCN 2018032006 | ISBN 9780838917725 (print : alk. paper)
Subjects: LCSH: Library science—Vocational guidance—United States. |
   Information science—Vocational guidance—United States.
Classification: LCC Z682.35.V62 W55 2018 | DDC 020.2373—dc23 LC record available at https://lccn.loc.gov/
   2018032006

Cover design by Karen Sheets de Gracia.
Text design and composition by Mayfly Design.

♾ This paper meets the requirements of ANSI/NISO Z39.48-1992 (Permanence of Paper).
Printed in the United States of America

23  22  21  20  19      5  4  3  2  1

*To Bud and Nancy Williams,*
*for your generosity of spirit,*
*loving-kindness,*
*and unconditional support.*
*I truly treasure you both!*

# Contents

# Foreword

CATHERINE HAKALA-AUSPERK

n one of the first career workshops I ever taught, I led attendees through a process to create a "Personal Strategic Plan" by asking them to identify their overarching professional goals, the specific objectives to reach those goals, and the concrete actions they could take to meet their objectives. I'll never forget one woman who came up to me afterward and said, "No one has ever offered me the time or opportunity to think about myself before! This was amazing!" Wow! Really? Never? At that moment, I had the strongest urge to send a one-word e-mail to her supervisor—"MOTIVATE!"

Motivate is exactly what career expert Caitlin Williams does on every page of *Be Opportunity-Minded: Start Growing Your Career Now*. In this book, Caitlin provides you with the framework, support, and direction to help you identify and pursue multiple opportunities to grow your career. You'll get to try out activities that will help you take a realistic look at where you are right now, identify what possibilities might be available to you going forward, and determine how you can move in your desired direction to grow your career. Caitlin suggests you blend play, creativity, and imagination together as you consider ways to leverage future trends and identify your own special opportunities within them.

I'd like to share my favorite parts of this book by highlighting some of the key points that Caitlin outlines.

- *Our careers keep changing, and our workplace does too.* Understanding current workplace and career-related challenges is essential in moving your career forward now and in the future. Yet finding a place to fit into our exciting, rapidly changing industry today is kind of like trying to throw a football through a swinging tire. Should you move toward archives or digitization or both? What's the difference? How about youth services or children's or teens' or tweens' or seniors' or adults'—and hey, where's the line between all of those anyway? School libraries around the nation are shuttering, so where do all those professionals go? This book outlines the trends in librarianship and information services and explains how knowing them can help you develop your own growth plan.

- *Success begins with understanding yourself.* With a thorough examination of your skills and abilities, Caitlin leads you to an honest and accurate picture of *you* as a professional. This may lead you to stay where you are or, perhaps, move somewhere else. Regardless of the direction you take, the information you gain through your self-assessment will help you better understand the range of skills, talents, and uniqueness you have to offer, which will allow you to stretch your options for growth.

- *Growth opportunities are everywhere.* Caitlin shows you a world of possibilities and offers practical tips on how to keep your momentum going. By being more opportunity-minded, as Caitlin suggests, you'll be able to think and act in new ways when it comes to moving your career forward.

As Caitlin notes in this practical guide, the poet Hugh Prather said, "There must be a better way to go through life than to do so kicking and screaming." I agree. If you do too, then read *Be Opportunity-Minded: Start Growing Your Career Now!*

# Acknowledgments

Thanks so much to all of you who helped make this book possible:

To Jamie Santoro, my awesome editor, whose wisdom, warmth, and serene demeanor I truly appreciate, and to my colleague Catherine Hakala-Ausperk for introducing us; to my ALA family, Lorelle Swader, Beatrice Calvin, Kimberly Redd, and Adriane Alicea; to my California family, Helen Choy, Stan Huang, Hannah Huang, and Ray Huang; to all the ALA conference attendees who have shared their career stories with me; and to my amazing, dear husband, Tom Mraz, whose never-ending support, caring, and superb cooking skills got me through!

# Introduction

Welcome!

As a library or information professional, you are a member of an exciting field that is—at this very moment—shifting and expanding in ways that we could not have predicted a decade or two ago. As a result of these changes, you may find yourself experiencing a whole range of feelings, concerns, or perhaps excitement about the future of librarianship and information services and about your own career. You may feel as committed as ever to your field and to making a difference. Or maybe you feel a bit apprehensive about just where you fit in your evolving field overall and how you can make a place for yourself to grow. It's also possible that you may feel bored, burned out, or stuck in your current position without any idea of how to move forward.

Regardless of where you find yourself on the fully-committed-and-passionate to disengaged-and-stuck continuum, you *can* grow your career from wherever you are right now!

Whether you're already employed in your field, seeking work, or just beginning your studies, I would like to help you move your career forward and deepen the satisfaction you get from your work. That's what this book is about.

All it takes is a willingness, on your part, to accept the invitation you'll read about in this introduction.

In my work as a career consultant, I have noticed that over the last decade, most library and information professionals, as well as library workers and advocates, are more and more frequently encountering a broader range of issues and multiple changes simultaneously, along with an increased thirst for continued learning and growth. Are you feeling these things too? See if any of the following three scenarios seem to fit you and your career:

Scenario #1: You find yourself continually looking to go deeper into your field through learning about new technologies, new products and services, or new ways that you can grow your expertise.

Scenario #2: You find yourself still quite committed to your field but are feeling a bit stifled, stuck, or bored because you haven't yet had the opportunity to spread your wings or take on new challenges and responsibilities.

Scenario #3: You've seen plenty of changes happening around you, or you know some are likely to appear on the horizon very soon, and you want to plan for a future in which you're in front of these changes rather than reacting to them.

Do any of these scenarios ring true for you? All of them are quite common for professionals who are serious about their careers. Regardless of age or career stage, we all tend to seek out the new when the familiar becomes too routine and feel drawn to things that suddenly intrigue us, develop a hunger to learn all we can about something we're passionate about, or simply gain new interests as we transition across our career lifespans. It's only natural—nothing remains the same forever. These feelings about your current situation don't imply that you should jump ship tomorrow, retire to some remote Greek island, or take up extreme snowboarding. They *do* suggest some hints, though, that perhaps you want to shake things up a bit, open yourself to new opportunities, and opt for a *growth mindset* (a phrase you'll read more about later in this book). To put it simply, you want to grow!

If any of these scenarios describe what you've been feeling lately (or if you've been experiencing some other urge to *stretch*), then consider this book a personal invitation—an invitation to say yes:

✓ yes to thinking and acting more expansively about your career options

✓ yes to seeking out and capitalizing on opportunities that will make your career even more meaningful and satisfying

✓ yes to watching your professional life unfold in exciting, challenging, and often pleasantly surprising ways

✓ yes to embracing the new career smarts

*If* you're willing to explore new possibilities rather than continue with the same-old, same-old ways you've worked up until now, *if* you're ready to truly take charge of your career future, and *if* you're up for the challenge and the excitement that professional growth can offer, then you're ready to accept this invitation to grow.

Why now? First and most importantly because you are a valued professional with more skills and experience than you probably imagine—and because you have the ability to shape your career future in more ways than you may think possible. Growth represents the next leap forward in your career trajectory.

Other important reasons to accept this invitation now? Even as time continues charging ahead, most of us are still accustomed to thinking of our careers in terms of the old rules that defined workplace success over the last three plus decades, and this type of thinking tends to limit our ideas about our options for growing our careers. Further, although the newer "rules" of the early 2000s appeared to broaden our older definitions of career success and satisfaction, they didn't help us think big enough to redefine our careers in ways that encourage proactive choices and actions to give more meaning and more options to our professional lives.

The reality is that in today's workplace, there are fewer opportunities for formal promotions, less money available for organization-sponsored continuing education, and less of a chance that you will remain with the same organization for your entire work life. As a result, there are more chances for boredom or disengagement in your current position if it's no longer challenging you—and more moments when you question the likelihood of reaching your true potential.

For these reasons, it's an excellent idea to consider *all* of your options for career growth. Your decision to grow professionally will offer you the best opportunities for a meaningful career where you can contribute your best efforts and truly make a difference. And choosing to grow professionally will place you in an excellent position to remain employable and valued.

So let's start with a very important question. Are you ready for it? Here it is:

*How many ways can you grow?*

No, this isn't a trick question. Obviously, you can grow *taller* (up to your maximum height). You can grow *heavier* in weight—or *lighter*. You can grow *older* (and presumably wiser) with age.

But what about the equally important dimensions of growth that have nothing to do with physical or chronological types of measurements? Those are the ones we'll be looking at in this book.

So look at the question again, and this time, let go of your thinking about the physical dimensions to growth and focus on all the other possible ways you can grow. Give yourself a few minutes to get creative (a sure sign of growth!) and see how many ways you can come up with. Jot down your notes here.

**Notes to Myself**

_____

_____

_____

_____

I'm hoping that the way you answered this question reflected your belief that there are no limits to the ways you can grow. Because that's the truth! You can grow in far more ways than you can imagine. And just *how* you can grow is what I'd like to share with you in this book because continuing to grow professionally represents the new career smarts.

Actually, the number of ways you can grow is ultimately determined by *you*—not by your job title, your official "place" on your organizational chart, the size of your system, or the size of the town you work in. The number of ways you can grow is not even determined by the fact that you're unemployed at the moment or you're employed for fewer hours than you'd like to be or you're in a role that appears to offer few chances to advance.

Choosing to grow is an individual decision. Of course, that decision can be encouraged by your supervisor or mentor, and it can be supported by others. But the ultimate decision to grow—and the actions that flow from that decision—starts with you.

If you choose to grow, will it guarantee you a new job title? A raise in pay? A better position at another organization? No—no guarantee. Will choosing to grow open up your options? Deepen your knowledge? Widen your skill base? Broaden your circle of influence? Increase your satisfaction with your work? The answer to these last five questions is yes—quite likely.

And depending on *how* you choose to grow—and how strategic and committed you are to the options for growth that you decide to pursue—it's likely you will start a process in motion that will open doors (and opportunities) that you weren't even aware of before. That's the magic of *Be Opportunity-Minded: Start Growing Your Career Now.* Once you learn how to determine which ways you want to grow, identify the opportunities, craft a growth plan, and strategically put your plan into action, you go from stuck to unstoppable.

Before going any further, let me share a bit about my background with you. My background, training, and experience since 1990 have been in the areas of career development and career coaching. Since 2000, I've had the good fortune to work with the American Library Association (ALA)'s Office of Human Resource Development and Recruitment. Twice a year, I participate in ALA's conferences (midwinter and annual). In the Placement Center at these conferences, I conduct career coaching for individuals attending the conferences who are looking for some career guidance. In fact, you and I may have already met at one of these sessions!

The laser-focused twenty-minute career coaching sessions I offer at the conferences cover how to find a job, choose a grad school, get along better with colleagues, move into leadership, get ready for retirement—and everything in between.

One big concern that is frequently mentioned by the people who come to see me in these sessions is this: *I'm stuck in my job—I've got nowhere to go from here!* This concern shows up in many variations, but the worry these individuals express is almost always the same: *I want to keep growing in my profession, but I just don't see how I can do it from where I am now!* Sometimes the person is stuck because there's no budget for professional development. Sometimes it's because the only position the person wants is the director's position—and the director isn't retiring anytime soon! Sometimes the person I'm coaching just wants to spread her wings. Or the person I'm working with says he wants to go deeper into the work he loves but isn't sure if his supervisor will let him. And frequently, those coming in for coaching use only three words to describe their situation: *Help! I'm stuck!*

That's why I wrote this book: to help professionals just like you get unstuck, remember why you joined this amazing field, deepen your sense of work satisfaction, and continue to make an even bigger difference. How? By expanding your range of potential career opportunities, understanding how to find these opportunities, and proactively pursuing the right opportunities to grow your career!

There are a few caveats that are important to mention here: If you feel like you are in "desperation mode" when it comes to your career—if you feel you need to make a change immediately, for whatever reason—then this book may not give you the type of suggestions that will help you change your situation quickly. If what you want is a quick change, it may help to seek out a career professional (a career counselor or career coach) and work with that person to resolve your immediate concern. This book can definitely give you ideas that will help you move your career in a direction that is more to your liking, but it will take time to formulate a plan and move into action.

If what you truly want at this moment is to quickly move into senior leadership, then this book will give you some sound suggestions that will help. However, it isn't meant to be an overnight quick-fix type of resource. Look to this book for dozens of ideas on building your knowledge, skills, and know-how; at the same time, also talk with your mentors, colleagues you trust and admire, and senior leaders whose opinions you value. Conversations with these individuals may offer you real-time help and feedback—and help you with your plan to move up. This book can nicely add to the resources and advice you get from them.

If you're burned out or dissatisfied with your work, then it makes good sense for you to address your burnout or the root of your dissatisfaction first. Burnout usually zaps our energy and makes it difficult to get motivated enough to do the things we know would make a difference in our careers. And if you're dissatisfied with your work, it may be really helpful to look to resources, including career coaches and counselors, to help you understand your dissatisfaction before you try to implement an action plan for growing your career. Still, some of the ideas in this book can help you take some actions to get yourself moving. See what works best for you.

And last, if you hope to grow by reading through this book but not putting your learning into action, then it might be an interesting read, but it's not likely to help you actually grow your career. So *do* read this book—but take it a step further. Put some (or all!) of the ideas into action. You'll be glad you did!

With those cautions addressed, I invite you to read on and start growing your career right now! Here is what you'll find in the chapters ahead that can make a difference in your career trajectory.

In chapter 1, we'll look at how the workplace keeps changing—and before you think you already know all there is to know about workplace changes, I urge you to take the time to read this section to truly understand what these changes mean for you and your career. I guarantee you'll learn something new that you can leverage in your own workplace.

In chapter 2, we'll explore how careers, in general, are changing. And more important, we'll examine how careers in library and information science (LIS), regardless of where you work or whether you're currently employed, are evolving. We'll take a closer look at what this information means for your field and for you—because this time, it's personal!

Chapter 3 shows you how all the workplace and career shifts that are happening can actually provide you with the opportunity to leverage these changes and turn them into growth opportunities.

Chapter 4 explains the most important "secret sauce" ingredient you'll need to take advantage of any growth opportunity. If you don't take the time and effort to uncover this secret ingredient, you won't be able to benefit from any action you take.

Chapter 5 gives you critical information about the trends that are just around the corner or just over the horizon. Information on trends gives you important clues about where and how your profession is growing and changing. Trends also give you ideas for identifying where growth opportunities will be on the rise. Additionally, chapter 5 offers some great ways to think like a futurist and envision your own possible opportunities for growth as a library professional. The exercises and ideas in this section will open a wider variety of possible paths you might want to explore and leverage.

In chapter 6, we'll take a closer look at growth opportunities from the perspective of identifying the best ones for you. You can't—and you shouldn't—pursue every opportunity you identify. But how do you know which ones are the best ones for you? This section will help you choose wisely.

In chapter 7, we'll explore the wide range of opportunities that are around you— *if* you know how and where to look and *if* you know what you're looking for! Don't worry—you'll get lots of good guidance here.

Chapter 8 focuses on the important next step: choosing the opportunities you want to pursue. Turning those opportunities into reality takes some work, and this section gives you a roadmap to help you make that happen.

In chapter 9, we'll look at ways to go beyond the basics of pursuing growth opportunities and explore possibilities for you to enhance your career and your life in more ways than you have imagined up until now.

Lastly, in the final section of this book, Your *Going for It!* Growth Plan, you'll learn just how to formulate a plan for growing your career and nurturing yourself and your career over the long term.

One final and very important point to mention here: if you are involved in any form of librarianship or information services—as an advocate, worker, or member of a profession closely aligned with this field—then you know quite well that the individuals and entities that support librarianship and information services do so from a vast array of backgrounds and a wide variety of job titles. It's likely that you also have some understanding of how much the field has transformed over the last decades. Given this transformation—and the fact that libraries and information organizations will continue to evolve—my intent in writing this book is to be as inclusive as possible in emphasizing the wide array of options for all who are a part of this truly amazing work. To do that, I have used the titles library professional, information professional, LIS staffer, and library worker interchangeably throughout the text. The ideas and suggestions for pursuing opportunities to grow one's career are open to all, and I encourage everyone who wants to gain expertise, experience more job satisfaction, and make more of a difference in their work to consider the possibilities that this book has to offer.

# CHAPTER 1

· · · · · · · · ·

# The Workplace Keeps Changing . . . *So What?*

O*f course* you know the workplace keeps changing—it's been doing so for decades and will, no doubt, continue to do so at an even faster pace going forward. No startling news there—no need to convince you of this fact. You know it all too well, and it's likely you live it every day. Still, it's interesting to note how many decades back people have been making pronouncements about workplace changes or warning us to be prepared. Here are some comments by noted authorities in a variety of fields on the topic of workplace change. Notice the similarity of themes dating back to the 1980s and going forward to the present day.

The first comment comes from Beverly Kaye, a career development specialist and astute observer of workplace shifts. In 1985, she wrote,

> It all used to be so simple. American workers selected a career area, educated themselves to pursue it, settled into an organization that could use their talents, worked to achieve higher rungs on the corporate ladder, and collected a gold watch at the mandatory 65-year retirement age. Myriad social, economic, and legal changes of recent years have radically disrupted this long-standing pattern. . . . Many individuals and organizations seem at a loss for means to anticipate and cope with the rapid evolution of their environments.[1]

And in the 1990s, futurists Edith Weiner and Arnold Brown noted,

> One important consequence of this rapidity of change [brought on by technology, industrialization and heightened marketplace competition] is the uncertainty

it creates. This uncertainty is felt most by employees who are more than halfway through their work life. And this is the first time new or recent college graduates believe that their education won't serve them for more than just a few decades. This is particularly true in technological fields . . . but it applies more and more to other disciplines as well.[2]

More recently, Seth Godin said it even more succinctly in 2015: "The death of the factory means that the entire system we have built our lives around is now upside down. This is either a huge opportunity or a giant threat."[3]

And even more recently, Lee Maxey, CEO of MindMax, commented on how workplace changes were being felt by new workers entering the workplace:

> Many companies don't know what their needs will be a few years from now. Not only are new jobs being created at a rapid pace but the environment within which grads will work is undergoing a metamorphosis with the evolution of collaborative robots, machine learning, drones and automated vehicles.[4]

Right about now, you may be saying, "So what? I already know this!" But stick with me for a moment longer. Because the most important "so what" of these changes is what they mean for you and your career. The bottom line? These changes—the global ones, national ones, technological ones, social ones, and especially the ones happening inside your own library—will have a direct impact on the future of *your* career. Sure, you know this on some larger, more general, macro level, but do you know it on a more personal, closer-to-home, micro level? Do you know how ongoing workplace changes will affect your daily work, your job, and your career prospects three to five years from now? Your answers to these questions represent the big "so what" challenges that are worth paying attention to.

Take a few moments now to reflect on the changes you've seen in your field and your workplace (if you're currently employed). If you're still in school, consider the topics your studies are addressing related to change. And if you're unemployed, note how these changes are affecting your own job search. Which of these changes stand out for you?

---

---

---

---

Keep your comments here in mind as we go forward.

At times, the speed and sheer amount of changes we see taking place around us can be so overwhelming that we'd like to ignore them for a while and just keep on doing what we've always done. It's a natural reaction to seek solid ground when things around us seem shaky. But it would be a mistake to turn our backs on these changes, pretend they have nothing to do with us, or assume they're just another round of fads that will eventually pass. They won't.

• • •

## Welcome to VUCA!

In case you're wondering, VUCA is not a planet in some distant galaxy. VUCA is much closer to home and happening right here and right now. It's happening in your city, your state, and the library or other workplace setting you're employed at—or the one you'd like to be employed at. VUCA, a strange-sounding word, is actually an acronym, first used by the US Army War College to describe conditions resulting from the end of the Cold War.[5] However, use of the acronym has expanded far beyond the military to almost every other entity and industry coping with change today. VUCA stands for "Volatility, Uncertainty, Complexity, and Ambiguity."[6] And it's a pretty good description of today's workplace, don't you think?

Of primary importance for our discussion is that VUCA means it's no longer business as usual for the work you do or the career aspirations you have. This doesn't mean you need to panic. It *does* mean, however, that you'll need to consider how best to go forward in a "VUCA-like" workplace.

Here's an important point to keep in mind. Although change in the workplace is nothing new, and people have been wringing their hands about it for a good, long time, the way in which we can respond to today's workplace-related changes is different. In the past, while changes happened, it was still "business as usual" when it came to how we conducted our career—our options for how to ride these waves of change were more limited. The "rules" of playing the career game were pretty much standard and agreed upon by most employers and workers. If changes resulted in your skills becoming outdated, you either looked for another job, often at lower pay, where you could still rely on your old skills to keep you employed for a while longer; you got demoted, did other types of work, and took a pay cut; or you went back to school (if you could afford it) and started all over again in a new field. In other words, you "settled for" what you could get or adjusted your expectations when workplace changes upset your world.

These responses to workplace changes in the past are not a foregone conclusion today. Now you can look at a wider range of options, whether it means staying in your current role and growing in place, finding new ways to make a difference as a professional in the field you love, transitioning to another role in your organization and learning new skills, or looking for new ways to mix and match your skill set in another type of workplace. It may even mean doing the very same thing you've always done but doing your work with a different mindset and purpose. Bottom line? You have more choices than you think—even in the midst of unrelenting change!

The trick to successfully managing change is to understand yourself exceedingly well, become savvy about what's needed in today's and tomorrow's workplace, and expand your own definitions of career, growth, advancement, meaning, and opportunity (all things we'll explore in the next chapters).

## The Work That Needs Doing (and How It Keeps Changing)

To become savvy about what the workplace needs right now—and how its needs keep changing—it's helpful to better understand "the work that needs doing" concept back through time.

The late William Bridges, an insightful author, astute observer of change, and workplace transition guru, wrote frequently on workplace changes. His book, *Job-Shift: How to Prosper in a Workplace without Jobs*, explored the changing nature of work and the workplace and discussed in powerful terms the impact of these changes on us as workers.[7]

We need to focus, he said, on "the work that needs doing" if we are to understand workplace changes and what we need to do to stay relevant and employable. I would add here that focusing on the work that needs doing also leads to more satisfaction and meaning in our professional lives. Let me give you some examples of what Bridges meant by "the work that needs doing" and how this type of thinking can help you grow your own career. Travel back in time with me (way back, actually) to the work of our ancestors in the past, and you'll understand more of what he meant by his comment.

Let's begin about seventy thousand or eighty thousand years ago, when people lived in a world focused on hunting and gathering. Picture them going about their daily lives, and you'll note that the work they engaged in centered around hunting, fishing, foraging for food, finding ways to prepare and cook that food, and defending against those scary predators hovering outside the family's cave-dwelling door. Those tasks represented *the work that needed doing* at that time.

Now travel forward to the point when people began settling down and turned to agriculture. For an agrarian people, tasks like domesticating animals, planting and harvesting crops, preserving them, building structures for storage and living, cooking, and making and mending clothes would all represent *the work that needed doing* at that time.

Next, leap ahead to the Industrial Revolution—a time when many individuals and families left the farm behind to look for new opportunities in factories in larger urban areas. Factory work called for different skills, marked by tasks that were more repetitive and more specialized, completed by a semiskilled workforce that typically worked on one machine and on only one part of the manufacturing process over and over again. Those tasks represented *the work that needed doing* in those circumstances.

Fast forward to the beginning of our more recent Information Age (recorded as beginning sometime around the mid-twentieth century), and you'll notice a shift in focus that moved work from tasks associated with traditional industry to those associated with computerizing information. Again, *the work that needed doing* changed, with less emphasis on physical labor and more emphasis on higher cognitive and decision-making skills. The requirements for entry into these new jobs shifted considerably as well. While work in the Industrial Age required manual skills and dexterity, as well as endurance and the ability to do repetitive work over a long period, work in the early days of the Information Age required technical skills to get hired—and the bar has continued to rise in terms of requirements since that time.

As we keep moving forward at an even more dizzying pace, computerization too has changed—morphing into its latest iterations; and new and emerging technologies have signaled the need for new skills, once again, to meet the demands of a new workplace. The bottom line of our tour through history? The work that needs doing has always been—and most likely, will always be—in flux. In many cases, we can't even be sure what that work will look like over the next decades when still-emerging technologies will take center stage. What we *can* be sure of is that to be successful going forward, old skills—like shoveling coal, cashiering, or operating a switchboard or fax machine—will need to be replaced or constantly upgraded to meet the demands of the new "work that *will* need doing."

Consider the new skills needed in *your* workplace. How have the key skills in your setting changed in the last five to ten years? If you're still in school, are you aware of the latest skills that will be in demand in the place you want to work? And if you're in job search mode, how has the bar been raised for *you* in terms of prospective employers' expectations about the skills you need to apply for open positions?

## Notes to Myself

_____

_____

_____

You may be wondering at this point about what all this "work that needs doing" focus has to do with a book about opportunities and—even more specifically—what it has to do with *your* career. Consider this: the professionals who make it a point to stay constantly updated and savvy about where their professions are going, and who understand the work that will be slowly fading in importance versus the work that will be growing in size and scope within their fields, will likely be the ones who are most employable, most job-ready, and most engaged in their work because they've chosen to take a stake in their futures. They are the ones who have chosen to stay on the cutting edge by being curious, skilled, and savvy about how growth will happen in their chosen fields. And they have put their research, their observations, and their ideas into action by seeking out and taking advantage of the best opportunities for growth that they can find. They have chosen to focus on the work that needs doing now and the work that will need doing tomorrow. This focus keeps them engaged, growing, and purposeful about how they shape their careers.

As Bill Bridges reminds us,

> People who see themselves only in terms of their job descriptions don't see what their strengths are. . . . Learn to see the world around you as markets with unmet needs. So many people look at change as a disruptive element, as something that takes something away from them. But change always creates unmet needs, so if people can refine their abilities to see the world, then they're always seeing possibilities and opportunities.[8]

Take a look around your workplace, or imagine the workplace you want to be in. What technologies are being introduced? Which technologies are no longer as useful as they once were? What customer demands, changes in demographics, or newly introduced services seem to be the most relevant? Which of these excite you? Make you curious? Have you wondering if they will still be important in five years (and what will take their place as needs change)? The answers to these questions all contain hints of the work that will need doing—and of the growth opportunities that may be just what you've been looking for.

Take a few moments to reflect on the questions raised in the previous paragraph. Whether you are employed or not, a student or a graduate, your answers here will guide you going forward.

## Notes to Myself

_____

_____

_____

_____

Here are some further words of wisdom that complement Bridges's comments on "the work that needs doing" and its relationship to change. These words come from the *Herman Trend Alert*, and they underscore what we've been looking at so far: "The keys to maintaining employability in the face of this transforming workplace, will be self-development, through enhancement of knowledge, skills, and attitudes, and the ability to adapt to continuous change."[9]

## What This Means for You

It's clear that the workplace is in continuous change mode. We know this to be true generally, and we know it to be true inside the field of librarianship as well. Here's the perspective of one author, writing in the *Futurist*, that lays out the challenges to those in the field:

> And now, the recent digitalization of the world is leading to even more dramatic transformations. Confronted with competition as knowledge bases, libraries must

redefine themselves, their services, business models and missions. In a world of edutainment and peer-to-peer information sharing, libraries could become not just the warehouses of knowledge, but also laboratories for creating it.[10]

Though these words come from an article that is more than four years old, the challenge to be relevant and at the forefront of providing cutting-edge services and programs that the article focuses on is just as true today.

Given our ever-evolving workplace, how do we best go forward? We'll be looking at a number of ideas for doing just that in upcoming chapters.

## The Bottom Line

Opportunities will be there for those willing to indulge their curiosity, stay alert to the work that needs doing now—and the work that will need doing in the future—and step up to the challenge of acquiring the right skills to make themselves employable and valued. Choosing to take these actions remains just as important whether you are a student, a new-to-the-field staff member, a seasoned professional, or a nearing-retirement worker.

## Notes

1. Beverly L. Kaye, *A Guide to Career Development Practitioners: Up Is Not the Only Way* (San Diego: University Associates, 1985).
2. Edith Weiner and Arnold Brown, *Insider's Guide to the Future* (Greenwich, CT: Boardroom Classics, 1997), 4–5.
3. Seth Godin, *Poke the Box: When Was the Last Time You Did Something for the First Time?* (New York: Portfolio, 2015), 4.
4. Lee Maxey, "Bridging the Last Mile," *Chief Learning Officer*, August 11, 2017, www.clomedia.com/2017/08/11/bridging-last-mile-close-skills-gap/.
5. Wikipedia.org, "Volatility, Uncertainty, Complexity and Ambiguity," https://en.wikipedia.org/wiki/Volatility,_uncertainty,_complexity_and_ambiguity/.
6. Nathan Bennett and G. James Lemoine, "What VUCA Really Means for You," *Harvard Business Review*, January–February 2014, http://hbr.org/2014/01/what-vuca-really-means-for-you/ar/pr/.
7. William Bridges, *JobShift: How to Prosper in a Workplace without Jobs* (New York: Perseus Books, 1994).
8. Caitlin Williams, "The End of the Job as We Know It," *Training & Development Magazine*, January 1999, 10.
9. Joyce Goia, "Employability in the New World of Work," *Herman Trend Alert*, July 12, 2017, www.hermangroup.com/alert/archive_7-12-2017.html.
10. Sohail Inayatullah, "Library Futures," *The Futurist*, November–December 2014, 25.

Here's an interesting exercise for you that emphasizes how our workplaces have changed.

Even the words and phrases that are used in today's workplace are different from jargon we used in the past. Take your best guess at matching up today's workplace jargon with the definitions for each word or phrase. Draw a line from a word or phrase in the left-hand column to its correct description in the right-hand column.

## Activity: Match Game

*(Answers are on next page)*

| Junk sleep | A chaotic situation |
| --- | --- |
| Nomophobia | Workers on the job but not functioning due to illness or other medical condition |
| 404 | Really tired |
| Open-collar workers | What to do when you really need some rest |
| Goat rodeo | When you fall asleep while still connected to your electronic devices |
| Cached-out | Fear of being separated from your mobile phone |
| Defrag | Workers who work from home / telecommute |
| Presenteeism | Don't have a clue |

## Answers to Match Game Quiz

**Junk sleep** = When you fall asleep while still connected to your electronic devices

**Nomophobia** = Fear of being separated from your mobile phone

**404** = Don't have a clue

**Open-collar workers** = Workers who work from home / telecommute

**Goat rodeo** = A chaotic situation

**Cached-out** = Really tired

**Defrag** = What to do when you really need some rest

**Presenteeism** = Workers on the job but not functioning due to illness or other medical condition

# CHAPTER 2

· · · · · · · · ·

# Our Careers Keep Changing Too!

o you agree with this quote from author Jon Acuff: "Careers are only difficult because they are constantly changing and we are not. We tend to hate change, despite the benefits it offers and ignore it, deny it, or fight it and become stuck"?[1] Do you hate change? Try to ignore it? Fight it? If you're like most people I know (myself included), the answer is probably "it depends." If the change is a big one, an unexpected and unpleasant one, or one that causes a lot of disruption, then it's likely that this kind of change wouldn't be welcomed. If it's a change that causes minimal interference, then it may be tolerated pretty well.

Yet we all know (*don't we?*) that like it or not, change *is* the new normal. And surprisingly, we seem to be growing more accustomed to the expectation of continuous change than we ever thought we would. But the way we go about accepting or adjusting to change can make a huge difference in the quality of our lives.

Poet Hugh Prather had it right when he said, "There must be a better way to go through life than to do so kicking and screaming."[2] He's right! Think for a moment about people you know who seem to complain about every change that comes along. It could be a change in toothpaste flavors, in the cost of postage stamps, in the reduced availability of their favorite dental hygienist, or the newest features on the mobile phone they just purchased. It could also be larger changes that may have a bigger impact on their lives. The point here is that these individuals' attitude toward change is always the same: rail against it, complain about it, get angry about it. Yet such an attitude rarely helps and too often puts us in a constant reactionary mode.

While it's true that we may not be able to do much about a particular change, we *can* do something about our attitude and our approach toward it. We can get in front of the change in several different ways: We can take a problem-solving approach or consider the impact of the change on us and then consider our options, or we can look for the hidden upside of the change we might not have noticed before. We can also brainstorm with others to determine a different way to approach the change. I'm not suggesting that making lemonade out of lemons is always the way to go with changes that aren't to our liking. But there are usually more options for dealing with change than "kicking and screaming" our way forward.

The same holds true for career and career-related changes that may impact us. These changes can be subtle (reduced money available for professional development) or more obvious and all-encompassing (salaries and promotion opportunities frozen for the foreseeable future). Or career-related changes can be ones that are more favorable. Suddenly, a promotion comes our way, or we're invited to chair an important work group project—an opportunity that we weren't expecting.

Either way, today's workplace will continue to surprise us as the speed of just about everything accelerates. And career-related changes will continue to rock us—guaranteed. Read on to get a handle on the implications of sweeping changes happening to careers everywhere and the smaller ones that may impact you, your career, and your field.

## It's a YoYo World Out There!

If VUCA (Volatility, Uncertainty, Complexity, and Ambiguity) describes our overall workplace landscape these days, then YoYo is a great acronym for describing our current (and future) *career* landscape. YoYo is another one of those acronyms that seems to neatly capture our current circumstances.

YoYo stands for "You're on Your own," at least when it comes to the management of your career. I first heard this term back in 2008, when it was used by Dr. Helen Harkness, a career consultant in Garland, Texas. Long gone are the days when your boss and the organization you worked for saw it as their responsibility to watch over your career progress, make certain you got steered toward the "right" career opportunities, or guided you toward key upward-bound positions.

As Harkness put it at the time,

> The job, as defined in the past, is dead. The path of loyalty to a company in return for 40-year employment, a gold watch at retirement, and then going home to wait to die is totally defunct.... We are responsible for balancing our own career on our current edge of chaos, constant change, complexity, and uncertainty. Though painful ... this can be the first step of growth, creativity, coherence, and order for our careers.[3]

Those past workplace realities, helpful as they might have seemed for those lucky enough to get some good guidance, essentially placed one's future career progress into somebody else's hands, which wasn't necessarily a good thing. It meant that you needed to follow someone else's script for a "successful career." And for those who weren't steered one way or another, it often resulted in feelings of powerlessness on the part of workers.

In spite of the downside of other people controlling your career, there are some workers, even today, who wish that someone else would take charge of their careers (relieving them of the career uncertainty plaguing most workplaces currently). But having others run your career life isn't ideal. Wouldn't *you* rather be the one to make your own career decisions? Shape your own career future? Sure, it's hard work and it doesn't always go in the direction you'd like it to, at least initially; however, it definitely opens up more opportunities than living out someone else's version of what's best for your career.

The message of self-responsibility for succeeding in the workplace seems to have gained momentum, with fewer people believing it's the organization who should be held responsible. A recent survey by the Pew Research Center makes it clear that a majority of Americans understand that career development and workforce readiness have become mostly DIY activities. As the Pew Center notes in its research, "Americans think the responsibility for preparing and succeeding in today's workforce starts with individuals themselves: Roughly seven-in-ten (72%) say 'a lot' of responsibility falls on individuals to make sure that they have the right skills and education to be successful in today's economy."[4]

With all these signals that the old style of career management is dead, what exactly does YoYo mean for *you*? Basically, it means that your career progression is based on your initiative, your decision making, and your actions (for the most part). Of course, there will always be those situations when your best efforts don't give you the career results you were hoping for. Or serendipity may step in and you find that you're invited to take on an awesome career role you couldn't possibly have predicted or prepared for. Whatever may happen, the most important point to understand is that YoYo means you take on the responsibility and the reward for shaping your career future. And if you hit a roadblock or need to take a detour, you can do so with more confidence because *you're* in the driver's seat—you are the one calling the shots, not someone else.

## What's Happening in LIS?

With changes going on in every workplace and affecting almost every field, it only makes sense that the LIS field would be affected as well. With that in mind, it's a good idea to take a closer look at how the LIS field itself along with the skills, knowledge, job titles, specializations, and emerging skill sets within the field have shifted. If you have a clearer picture of where librarianship is going and what that might mean for your ability to anticipate and prepare for these shifts, it's easier to know where to focus as you move your career forward.

One good place to begin is to look at ways that library and information professionals are currently using their skills and training in an ever-widening range of positions and work settings. Such information offers hints about new and emerging workplace needs and points toward options and required skills you may want to consider as you look ahead to possible opportunities on the rise. And you can be sure that newer and emerging skill sets and work settings will only increase in number going forward. If you can get a good grasp of the skills that are—and will be—in demand, you will be better able to consider what you'll need to have in your skill-set toolbox to remain current and valued in your field. The following research offers some good ideas.

## Job Titles, Opportunities, and Specialized Skills on the Rise

A 2018 study done by San Jose State University (SJSU)'s School of Information, titled "MLIS Skills at Work: A Snapshot of Job Postings," is the latest version of their annual report and analysis that provides a snapshot of the latest career trends for library and information science professionals. The following list (gathered from job postings) includes representative job titles—many of which include the word *librarian,* but others that do not. The report notes that these titles are "indicative of the diverse ways LIS knowledge is being applied."[5]

✓ Archivist
  ○ Archive Assistant
  ○ Archival Digitization Specialist
  ○ Corporate Archivist
  ○ Curator of Archives
  ○ Digital Archivist
  ○ Lead Processing Archivist
✓ Cataloging
  ○ Cataloger
  ○ Cataloging and Metadata Librarian
  ○ Music Cataloger
  ○ Principal Cataloger and Linked Data Strategist
✓ Communications Specialist/Writer
✓ Conflicts Analyst
✓ Content Developer

✓ Curator of Oral Histories
✓ Data Collection Manager
✓ Digital Asset Management
✓ Digital Initiatives Program Manager
✓ Document/Data Control Analyst
✓ Due Diligence/Fraud Research Specialist
✓ Emerging Technology Librarian
✓ Information Technology Specialist
✓ Knowledge Center Head of Operations
✓ Librarian
  ○ Access Services Librarian
  ○ Business Librarian
  ○ Children's/Youth Librarian
  ○ Medical Librarian
  ○ Reference Librarian

- ○ Special Collections Librarian
- ○ Technical Librarian
- ✓ Library Product Manager
- ✓ Litigation Intelligence Analyst
- ✓ Social Media Specialist
- ✓ Technology Hub Administrative Staff
- ✓ User Experience (UX) Lead
- ✓ Workflow Analyst/Programmer

*(SJSU School of Information 2018, 12)*

The SJSU School of Information study goes a step further and identifies the skills that seem to be the most in demand right now—and in the near future as well. According to the SJSU School of Information Study, the following skills were mentioned most often by employers. As you read through them, you might want to rate yourself on how well your own skill sets match up with these.[6]

- ✓ Communication/Interpersonal Skills
- ✓ Collaboration/Team Work
- ✓ Training/Instruction/Developing or Delivering Content
- ✓ Reference/Research
- ✓ Electronic Resources, Web Applications, and Software
- ✓ Integrated Library Systems/ Software/Database/Technology Experience
- ✓ Independence/Time Management / Multi-Task/Detail
- ✓ Best Practices/Trends in Library Services/Library Management
- ✓ Customer/User Service
- ✓ Basic Computer/Internet Skills
- ✓ Analysis/Critical Thinking/ Problem Solving
- ✓ Diversity Sensitivity
- ✓ Organizational

*(SJSU School of Information 2018, 13)*

Finally, we can take one step even further and review the more specialized skills that are in demand according to the SJSU report. The list that follows was compiled by looking at specialized skills/duties mentioned most often in job listings that the study's authors reviewed. Once again, as you review the following list, note which ones reflect your own strengths. Remember too that this list represents the findings from one report. Your own particular strengths or strong areas of interest may not be represented here. However, as you reflect on your own strengths and skill sets, consider their marketability and relevancy in today's workplace (or the one you wish to enter)—whether that is a traditional library or a nontraditional work setting—and what you may need to do to make certain you are as up-to-date in your own area of interest and expertise.[7]

- ✓ Accessibility/Assistive Technologies
- ✓ Art Curation
- ✓ Audio/Visual Preservation
- ✓ Business Analysis
- ✓ Classical Music/Music History
- ✓ Communications/Design
- ✓ Competitive Intelligence
- ✓ Copyright Expertise
- ✓ Digital Humanities
- ✓ GIS

- ✓ Grant Writing/Management
- ✓ History Research
- ✓ Instructional Design
- ✓ Legal Research
- ✓ Literacy
- ✓ Marketing/Media Strategy
- ✓ Medical Device Regulatory Compliance
- ✓ Rare Materials Preservation
- ✓ Scholarly Publishing
- ✓ Science/Health/Pharmaceutical Research
- ✓ Social Media
- ✓ Statistical Software
- ✓ Storytelling
- ✓ Systems Administration

*(SJSU School of Information 2018, 14)*

You may also want to review other reports that note the skills, knowledge, and areas of specialization that will be important over the next ten plus years. For instance, take a look at the fascinating report compiled by Pearson and Nesta, and be sure to look through the section labeled "The Top 10 Occupations Predicted to Experience Increased Demand through 2030," which includes librarians, curators, and archivists.[8] Another helpful source for you is "Placements & Salaries 2017: Librarians Everywhere," put together by *Library Journal.*[9] Also check out the *Occupational Outlook Handbook* (OOH), which posted the following comment regarding libraries and librarians: "Communities are increasingly turning to libraries for a variety of services and activities. Therefore, there will be a continuous need for librarians to manage libraries and help patrons find information."[10] The OOH offers a wealth of information related to salaries, training, and job outlook under the heading of librarians.

There is one important concern I want to point out here. Whenever some person or group makes predictions or forecasts about the future—in terms of what jobs will be in demand, what industries will be growing, what workplaces will look like, or what skills will be needed—there will be some who disagree.

At times, their disagreement may stem from cynicism about the likelihood of new jobs that will open up or the benefits of gaining new skills. Some individuals continue to struggle to find new work, despite their best efforts. And so it is understandable that they may have some misgivings about any news of new jobs they can apply for. The same holds true for those who don't want to hear about the necessity of more new skills that will be needed after they've invested so much in gaining skills in the past. But the emphasis here is not on how many new jobs there will be. My hope is that in giving you information about what the data and trends show (and trends are good indicators of shifts that are already being observed), along with reports showing evidence of what employers are looking for, you'll have good information about where growth opportunities are likely to be popping up—and that will help you focus your efforts as you move your career forward.

To get an additional perspective on how LIS workers' jobs—and the skills needed to do these jobs—are changing, let's zero in on one specific specialty area of work:

special librarianship. Kim Dority, an information professional and author, notes that while traditional librarianship (and special librarianship) jobs are decreasing in number, the opposite is true for new work opportunities. For example, as she explains it, "Special librarianship jobs are increasingly transforming into embedded or integrated information professional roles, and the requisite skills are morphing into previously uncharted territories such as digital asset management, data gathering, organizing, analyzing and synthesizing, and social media marketing."[11]

If you were to look further into other specializations within librarianship, chances are very good that you would see something similar: older job titles and tasks morphing into new ones—with the work often being done in new locations, in new ways, or with additional new skill sets.

## The Realities of "Career" in 2020

So far, we've looked at how work, workplaces, job titles, and skills are changing. At the same time, our ideas about career, career progression, advancement, and growth are also shifting. In decades past, each of these words had a more limited definition—and a generally accepted belief that fewer paths were available. Today, our understanding of all things related to career development is more nuanced and more a matter of personal and subjective definitions rather than a universally accepted and narrow definition. In other words, how each of us define career and advancement is more important than some generic, one-size-fits-all definition. Let's take a closer look at these words and how a broader view of each of them benefits you today.

### Career

*Career* is a word that has had dozens of iterations over the past decades—and it has also held multiple meanings for individuals as they approach their work lives. Some definitions of career are limited to one's current work; others distinguish *career* from *job* by noting that a career is something you commit to over time that leads to advancement, in the form of an increase in wages, titles, or responsibility. A job, on the other hand, according to this thinking, is a series of unrelated positions you hold— someplace you go each day to do the work you need to do to pay the bills. Other definitions of *career* include work done over a lifetime, which may involve several related positions. And when it comes to personal meanings that we ascribe to the word *career*, it's often in the context of whether we believe our "career" is successful or not. Or it's about the judgments that others place on *their* estimations of whether we've made it in what *they* consider to be an appropriate or lucrative enough career. Seems like the word *career* can carry a lot of baggage!

However, in our current workplace, and especially as we move toward 2020 and beyond, *career* needs a more encompassing definition. Many researchers and practitioners are looking at *career* from a much broader perspective at the present time. The meaning that one's work holds for an individual (such as the ability to be of service to others, the ability to help others communicate more effectively, or the ability to help organizations run more effectively) may be more important than one's job title, level in the organization, or work in a particular industry.

Similarly, others have suggested that we should incorporate into our definition of *career* how people find meaning in their work and make sense of their lives through their work. This seems especially important today, when there is often minimal job security, constant change, and pervasive uncertainty about whether one will have the chance to pursue the exact "career" one has studied and prepared for.

If you believe you are making a difference in your work, if you derive satisfaction from your lifelong commitment to educating others, or if you find contentment in contributing to work teams that are alleviating poverty or disease, or other valuable endeavors, that may color how you define "career" for yourself. Or your definition of *career* may be one that gives you opportunities for creativity, ongoing independence, or the chance to lead. The important point is that *you* are the one defining *career* for yourself.

What do you think? How do you define *career* for yourself? Let go of how *career* has been defined in the past and how organizations may define it—and also let go of how your friends or family may define it. Instead, consider your own definition of *career*. There are no wrong answers here. Just be sure you are defining *career* based on what it means to you in your life—and what you'd like it to look like going forward.

### Notes to Myself

_____

_____

_____

_____

### Career Progression

*Career progression* is a phrase that has certainly undergone a number of changes. For the several past decades, career progression, at least from the employers' perspective, meant following clearly marked career paths that led to advanced titles on a particular career "track." Individuals too felt that they were (or weren't) progressing depending on the number of promotions they received or the number of people they managed.

More recently, though, employers have embraced a broader definition of career progression to involve not only upward advancement but also lateral moves if they improve a worker's skill set and better prepare that person for taking on a higher-level position at some future point. In an article in *Chief Learning Officer*, author Katie Kuehner-Hebert describes how one employer chose to advocate for an expanded view of career progression:

> To keep them engaged—and from leaving—Don Kraft, Genentech's director of HR career and learning, said leaders had to change the existing mindset that up was the only way to go. "Career opportunities can be lateral, they can be vertical, they can be a job assignment, they can be working on a global project for a period of time, and they can even be developing in your current role over a period of time."[12]

*Career progression* from the individual's perspective has undergone similar changes—moving from an older view of career progression as a series of upward promotions leading to senior-level positions to the more current view of positions/roles/assignments that give an individual a broader and deeper range of skills and know-how. And the direction that career progression takes is much more varied and with fewer negative judgments by oneself or others than before. Author Beverly Kaye sums it up in the title of her newly revised book, *Up Is Not the Only Way*.[13] The bottom line? Career progression is multidirectional.

### Career Advancement

The meaning of *career advancement*, another phrase similar to *career progression*, has also changed. Although you'll find that the traditional definition of *advancement* as "promotion in rank or standing," according to Reference.com,[14] is considered by many to still hold true, you'll also see other perspectives that question our older assumptions about this phrase and broaden our thinking about this term.

Author Beverly Kaye and coauthor Julie Giulioni are spot-on when they describe advancement in this way: "Advancement today means moving forward and toward a very personal definition of career success."[15]

What hasn't changed in our look at all things career-related, however, is the ongoing requirement for gaining relevant skills and knowledge. Or maybe that requirement has changed too—in the direction of raising the bar even higher on the importance of continually increasing one's skill set. Consultant and author Marshall Goldsmith notes the challenge quite succinctly in the title of his book, *What Got You Here Won't Get You There.*[16] We'll look at this issue of upskilling more closely in the next chapters, where you'll have the opportunity to assess your own level of skill and knowledge.

## What Happened to the Career Ladder?

As we've already seen in the not-so-distant past, career progression and advancement looked a lot like a ladder that one would climb a rung at a time. Up was the direction you aimed for—taking on more senior levels of responsibility, titles, and the number of people reporting to you. Management was the direction most serious professionals were headed. Whether it was the corporate ladder, organization ladder, or academic ladder, the key word here was *ladder*.

As you look at the drawing on the right, you'll notice that there isn't a lot of room on each rung for more than one or two people. And that ladder could become a bit more treacherous if any particular rung happened to be missing or broken, thus making the climb harder!

## The Career Lattice

In our current workplace climate, the metaphor of the ladder no longer fits. Some have suggested a lattice with webbing, still somewhat evenly spaced like a ladder but with room to move back and forth, up and down, or even diagonally to traverse it.

Others have suggested a mobile phone, one that you can add apps to as the situation dictates—you simply add more apps to update skills, gain more experience, add contacts, and so on as you traverse your career. And still others have suggested an airplane's cockpit, with an array of buttons and levers that you would manipulate as career circumstances change.

### *Done Any Bouldering Lately?*

If you're navigating today's workplace, then the answer to the question posed above, "Have you done any bouldering lately?," would be a "yes"—at least metaphorically.

Bouldering, according to Wikipedia, is "a form of rock climbing that is performed on large boulders, small rock formations or artificial rock walls, without the use of ropes or harnesses."[17] And while it certainly doesn't involve a ladder, it does involve thoughtful movement: both up and down as well as back and forth and diagonally, requiring full concentration and engagement to be done successfully. While you may not see yourself as a rock climber, you have to admit that skillful bouldering does sound a lot like what is required for successfully progressing in one's career today!

I was curious about bouldering as a metaphor for career progression in our current workplace, so I spent some time with San Francisco Bay Area bouldering enthusiast Hannah Huang, who has been climbing for five years now, to learn more about the techniques involved in this popular sport.

In our interview, I asked Hannah about her interest in bouldering and also about some of its challenges. Here's an excerpt from that interview:

*Caitlin*: How does a person begin bouldering? Is it an easy sport at first?

*Hannah*: Everyone starts out not doing very well in the beginning. Some people with a lot of upper body strength may find it easier at first, but that's not sustainable over time. Also you just learn how to move your body and it gets easier. You use different body positioning. It's not all about pull-ups. It's too much to do without balance and using your legs.

*Caitlin*: How does a person get better at it?

*Hannah*: Practice. Patience. There's a grading system based on difficulty level (beginning with v-0 [easiest] and going up to v-17). Regardless of where people are in their bouldering skills, when they go to the gym, they use the lower-level climbs (on the range of level of difficulty) to warm up first.

*Caitlin*: What do you do when you hit a plateau?

*Hannah*: For a while, I was 4 to 5, and it took a long time to jump from 6 to 7. You work on climbs you're stuck on (called "projecting a climb"; it's your project) by practicing the types of moves you struggle with. For instance, there are different types of moves: crimps, pinches, slopers, mantling (where you pull yourself up and then you push up—that can be hard for me sometimes). So you practice. And also, trying things above your level. People also do pull-up workouts/training exercises (hang board, system board, moon board) to get stronger. It also depends on your style. Some climbs are a lot easier for me, even if they are technically hard. Some climbs are rated lower but are harder for me. So you just try different climbs—training different muscles/working on movements that are challenging for you.

*Caitlin*: How do you plan your climb (beyond determining the level of difficulty)?

*Hannah*: Each path to a climb is called a problem. Sometimes, when people are trying to do something that's hard for them or above their level, they do a "project" on their problem, which means they may have to work on it multiple times or in multiple sessions to achieve their goal.

So in these instances, you do the climb, and if you fall, you start up again from where you fell, and if it's scary, maybe you just practice one move. Or you do half of the move, try it multiple times, or try different hand placements. You basically try a number of things.

*Caitlin*: Overall, what does it take to succeed in bouldering?

*Hannah*: Patience. Practicing. Sometimes moving on and coming back later. Sometimes you get stuck on something—maybe you're "not there" at that moment. Then you move on and try something else to boost your confidence—or try something more your style. At times, it's hard because a lot of people are watching you, so it can be intimidating. But then you just decide to go for it.

*Caitlin*: If you're hiking, you just keep climbing vertically—more or less—moving one foot in front of the other on trails. In bouldering, it seems more complex. Which do you enjoy more?

*Hannah*: In general, bouldering is not the most efficient way up if you're trying to get from point A to point B. Sometimes the moves are hard and you go in what seems to be a weird direction; for instance, you move right, then left, then right again—back and forth. It's not linear. On trails, you're not zigzagging on the trails.

Sometimes in climbing it seems so ridiculous how much effort you put in to do a few moves. Like putting your foot up and doing a bunch of little moves just to move one foot. It's sometimes how the problem is set, and sometimes it's because I'm short and I need to do "micro beta." These are little moves, sometimes using footholds or weird beta so that I can make the same move as someone else who is taller/stronger could do in one.

But it's fun to figure out different problems and figure out different ways to do things, and it's probably challenging in different ways than hiking. For bouldering, you definitely get to a point where something is very hard and being able to get past that and surprise yourself by getting stronger and by trying again—it's a good feeling.[18]

Here are some lessons I picked up from Hannah during our interview that seem particularly useful as we think of growing our careers today through the lens of bouldering:

- We can't rely on just one skill or strength—that's not sustainable over time or in different circumstances. We have to learn and build up other strengths and skills to fit the requirements of changing workplace challenges.

- Growing our careers takes patience and practice. It doesn't happen overnight. To be successful, we can't jump in over our heads. There are skill sets, strengths, and areas of knowledge we need to gain first—and then we need to continue growing them over time.

- We all get stuck in our careers at times. Getting stuck represents an opportunity to become better at areas that may need improvement. It's also an opportunity to consider different ways to grow or different approaches. And getting stuck may offer opportunities that represent small risks—where we step out of our comfort zone to try something new.

- There will be times when we fail at something we try to do (at least at first). And there will be times when we may feel intimidated by others. What we need to remember is that each of us will traverse our own career using different methods and routes (very few of them are linear). The point is to keep moving. And we can often surprise ourselves by how strong we become along the way!

We've covered an amazing range of changes in this chapter—and you might be feeling your thoughts spinning with what all this means to your career. I know you've seen headlines, read articles, or listened to podcasts that highlighted these changes. It's one thing to take all this information in as just another part of our evolving world. But it's quite another thing to reflect deeply on just what all these changes truly mean for you, your profession, and your own career aspirations on a day-to-day basis. Don't worry—the chapters coming up are devoted to how you can truly benefit from all these changes (aka, our "new normal").

Before you go on to chapter 3, consider these words of wisdom from author Kim Dority:

> By facing these realities, you'll be much better prepared to take maximum advantage of what some are calling today's career chaos, also known as the new normal. You'll realize you have many more choices than might have seemed evident at first glance, and you can start developing the skills and mind-set necessary to place yourself in the path of opportunity.[19]

## That Was Then. This Is Now.

Here's an interesting look at an "old" (circa 1939) definition of one type of librarianship. It's especially interesting when compared to a similar job title described online much more recently. I think the comparison will make you smile!

Description of Librarian II—comparable to Audiovisual Librarian
*(from Dictionary of Occupational Titles, 1939)*

Manages a library in a motion picture studio in which he places film for future reference; keeps complete catalog index of every film in library by film title or scene reference; cuts out pieces of a positive film and pieces the film together with a hand-powered sprocket machine.[20]

Now check out this job description for a similar position in 2012:

Description of Department Head, Audiovisual Services Position
*(from WebJunction.org, circa 2012)*

Plans, organizes and supervises the operations and services of all audiovisual services of the Library, including the acquisition and maintenance of materials and equipment, the training and development of staff in the use of equipment and in the knowledge of audiovisual services and opportunities, and leads in direct services to patrons; and coordinates activities with other unit heads. Assists patrons planning audiovisual programs on content, utilization and technical matters. Provides audiovisual development and training opportunities for all staff members. Oversees maintenance of audiovisual equipment. Serves as library's representative to AV-oriented professional associations, advisory groups and meetings.[21]

## Notes

1. Jon Acuff, *Do Over: Make Today the First Day of Your New Career* (New York: Penguin, 2017), 19.
2. Hugh Prather, *Notes to Myself* (Moab, UT: Real People Press, 1972).
3. Helen Harkness. "The YoYo Model for Your Future Career: You're On Your Own," *Career Planning and Adult Development Journal* 24, no. 2 (Summer 2008): 10.
4. Pew Research Center, "The State of American Jobs," Social and Demographic Trends, October 6, 2016, www.pewsocialtrends.org/2016/10/06/the-state-of-american-jobs/.
5. San Jose State University School of Information, "MLIS Skills at Work: A Snapshot of Job Postings," *Annual Report*, 2018, http://ischool.sjsu.edu/sites/default/files/content_pdf/career_trends.pdf.
6. Ibid.
7. Ibid.
8. Hasan Bakhshi, Jonathan Downing, Michael Osborne, and Philippe Schneider, "The Top 10 Occupations Predicted to Experience Increased Demand through 2030," in *Future of Skills: Employment in 2030* (London: Pearson and Nesta, 2017), www.nesta.org.uk/sites/default/files/the_future_of_skills_employment_in_2030_0.pdf.
9. Suzie Allard, "Placements & Salaries 2017: Librarians Everywhere," *Library Journal*, October 17, 2017, https://lj.libraryjournal.com/2017/10/placements-and-salaries/2017-survey/librarians-everywhere/#_.
10. US Department of Labor, "Librarians," in "Job Outlook," *Occupational Outlook Handbook*, last modified July 2, 2018, www.bls.gov/ooh/education-training-and-library/librarians.htm#tab-6/.
11. G. Kim Dority, *Rethinking Information Work: A Career Guide for Librarians and Other Information Professionals*, 2nd ed. (Santa Barbara, CA: Libraries Unlimited, 2016), xiv.
12. Katie Kuehner-Hebert, "Career Advice Key to Post-growth Development," *Chief Learning Officer*, November 4, 2014, www.clomedia.com/2014/11/04/career-advice-key-to-post-growth-development/.
13. Beverly Kaye, Lindy Williams, and Lynn Cowart, *Up Is Not the Only Way: Rethinking Career Mobility* (San Francisco: Berrett-Koehler, 2017).
14. Reference.com, "What Is the Definition of Career Advancement?," www.reference.com/business-finance/definition-career-advancement-8827c0f5fd4e06d6/.
15. Beverly Kaye and Julie Giulioni, *Help Them Grow or Watch Them Go: Career Conversations Employees Want* (San Francisco: Berrett-Koehler, 2012), 64.
16. Marshall Goldsmith, *What Got You Here Won't Get You There* (New York: Hyperion Books, 2007).
17. Wikipedia.org, "Bouldering," https://en.wikipedia.org/wiki/Bouldering.
18. Hannah Huang, phone interview with the author, November 2017.
19. Dority, *Rethinking Information Work*.
20. The Job Analysis and Information Section Division of Standards and Research, *Dictionary of Occupational Titles*, pt. 1, *Definitions of Titles* (Washington, DC: US Government Printing Office, 1939), 547.
21. WebJunction.com, "Audiovisual Librarians Job Descriptions," last modified March 21, 2012, www.webjunction.org/documents/webjunction/Audiovisual_Librarian_Job_Descriptions.html.

# CHAPTER 3

· · · · · · · · ·

# Capitalize on Changes
# Starting Right Now

Right about now, you might be wondering, *How do I move my career forward in a complex world where it's often difficult to know what's next?* The answer is *not* to look for the newest shiny object on the horizon and go after it because it won't stay shiny for long; and it's soon likely to be replaced by the *next* big thing. Most of us have felt the pull of some new technology, trendy approach, or awesome idea—imagining that this new "thing" will take us where we want to go and be the answer to our uncertainties. And yes, for a while that may be true—but what do we do after that glitzy new technology fades and gets replaced by another? Or when the latest approach to management is challenged and found to be not quite so effective? Or when the people we serve present us with yet another new challenge? It's quite likely that the shiny new object we latched onto won't get us too much further along.

Back to the question that started this chapter: What's the best way to move your career forward? There are several approaches to moving your career forward that are worth trying—perhaps you already have some sort of system that helps you stay on the cutting edge and keeps your career well-oiled and humming along. If so, great! I encourage you to continue using what works for you. I also encourage you to read through this chapter to see how you can add some tools to your toolbox that you can consistently use to remain relevant and valued.

If you have some uncertainty about how to go forward with your career, then you'll be joining a very large number of professionals who are also expressing this same uncertainty. This chapter is focused on helping you look at these concerns, and it offers you an approach that can be used for the life of your career—it has no expiration date. It will take both reflection and action on your part—and chances are good that you're already using some parts of this approach. So you need not worry that you're going to be starting from scratch. I'm going to suggest that you leverage what you're already doing—and add some new ideas that will offer you even more value.

If you've read this far into *Be Opportunity-Minded: Start Growing Your Career Now*, it's likely you've already accepted the invitation to grow your career. Now that you've reviewed the many changes and challenges in our ever-evolving workplace, where career development and career progression look a whole lot more like a climbing wall than a ladder, you're probably curious about how you can begin (or continue) to strategically grow your career. I believe you can do this by *pursuing the right opportunities going forward.*

I want to emphasize this point because it is the linchpin that makes everything else work. For the remainder of this book, and for all you do going forward in your career, I invite you to *think opportunities*. Where others may see a chaotic workplace full of obstacles, limits, and "not-possibles," others see the changes and challenges we're undergoing right now in our careers and workplaces as *possibilities* that contain career-growth opportunities. You can see and act on those opportunities too, if you're willing to take on the task of identifying the *right* opportunities, pursuing them, and getting the most out of them. That is what the remainder of this book is about. Don't underestimate the value of choosing to pursue career-growth opportunities as a long-term career-smart strategy. It's a strategy that will serve you well, whether you're employed or not, whether you're just starting out or nearing the *end* of your career. It's not a once-and-done type of activity; rather, it's a mindset, with a bias toward both reflection and action. And it's one that builds momentum so that the more you do it (choose to pursue growth opportunities), the more benefits you'll realize.

The good news is that it's quite likely that you are already doing it right now, whether you're aware of it or not. You're taking a class, reading a book, or registering for a webinar to learn the latest version of a new technology that will help you in your work. Or you are part of a committee that is advocating on an important issue. If these sound like activities that you are already involved in, then you'll find materials in the chapters to come that will help you make the most of the opportunities that you're already pursuing and provide suggestions for strategically doing more to grow your career.

If you're not pursuing growth opportunities right now, that's OK too. Life circumstances can sometimes put other issues that need attention on the front burner first before you're able to turn your attention to pursuing professional growth. If that's the case, the current moment is a great time to consider how you'd like to incorporate growth opportunities into your career plans going forward, when you have the time and energy. Either way, now is a good time to thoughtfully and strategically consider how you best want to capitalize on what you've read so far and what you already know so that you are ready to launch your growth plan starting as soon as the time is right for you.

# A Closer Look at Career-Growth Opportunities

Let's begin with some background on what growth opportunities *are* and what they *are not*, along with some good reasons for pursuing them—and the possible downsides if you don't.

An *opportunity*, as I'm highlighting it in this book, refers to "an appropriate or favorable time or occasion, a situation or condition favorable for attainment of a goal, or a good position, chance or prospect, as for success," according to Dictionary.com.[1]

An opportunity can be represented by a particular moment or a set of circumstances that presents itself. It can be an activity or even a change in one's thinking or beliefs that offers a different perspective.

# Think about Different Ways of Looking at Opportunities

## Career-Growth Opportunities

The main topic of this book, career-growth opportunities, represents activities, assignments, or experiences that have the possibility of helping you grow your career through deepening (or broadening) your skills, knowledge, and savvy in areas that may or may not be the focus of your current position or job responsibilities. (For the remainder of this book, I'll be referring to them as growth opportunities, learning opportunities, or simply opportunities.) Such opportunities may include areas in which you already have some knowledge and skills but want to gain more expertise. They may also be in areas that are tangential to your current work, or they may represent aspirational goals you have. In all instances, they represent chances for you to *try* something new, *learn* something new, *experience* something new—or offer you a new take on something you already know. Bottom line? They stretch you beyond what you know and what you do right now—they may even stretch your sense of yourself as a professional in your field.

Growth opportunities, as I'm describing them here, include three categories: professional development, personal development, and a shift in mindset. Here is a brief description of each:

## Professional Development

According to the *Oxford Dictionary*, professional development is "the development of competence or expertise in one's profession; the process of acquiring the skills needed to improve performance in a job."[2] Professional development can include formal learning in educational venues such as classes, degree programs, or certificate programs, as well as journal and magazine reading and participation in webinars, podcasts, associations, or committees. You get the picture—anything you would normally think of as opportunities to learn more about your field, your position (or ones you aspire to obtain), or the chance to increase your skills or your knowledge. Pursuing these types of growth opportunities often provides new learning that you can often put to use quickly and demonstrates commitment on your part to your own career growth.

Professional development can also include opportunities that may take other forms, such as mentoring (being mentored or mentoring others), job shadowing, job rotations, internships, and similar activities. We'll talk more about all these options in chapter 7.

In terms of its value, professional development offers a whole host of benefits to help you grow your career. As Beatrice Calvin, manager of professional development at the ALA describes it, professional development opportunities can

- ✓ help you gain new skills and/or knowledge;
- ✓ keep you up-to-date on current trends;
- ✓ help you keep your skill level from becoming outdated;
- ✓ increase your marketability;
- ✓ prove to potential employers (if you should become unemployed) that you value lifelong learning through your actions;
- ✓ lead to new interests, a new career path, or new passion;
- ✓ reenergize you;
- ✓ improve the possibility of getting a salary increase;

- ✓ expand your current job responsibilities—adding new creativity and excitement to your work;
- ✓ open possibilities for a career change;
- ✓ improve job satisfaction;
- ✓ make you the "go-to" person that people rely on for your knowledge and expertise;
- ✓ keep your mind sharp and focused;
- ✓ enhance cognitive abilities;
- ✓ keep you from feeling intimidated by younger professionals;
- ✓ enrich all areas of your life; and
- ✓ allow you to make connections and meet new people.

Want any more reasons to pursue professional development opportunities? Calvin adds an additional point that we may sometimes forget—although it's a very critical one that we need to consider. She notes,

> When I think about the benefits of life-long learning, I find that there is one benefit that I consider to be the greatest: the boost or increase to an individual's self-confidence. When you continue to gain new skills and learn new information, your

competence and level of expertise tends to increase. As you master various knowledge areas, you will slowly build your confidence. You will walk in this confidence. You believe in yourself and portray yourself as a professional. Others notice this confidence and treat you with a certain level of respect. Having a healthy level of self-confidence can reduce anxiety while producing an individual who is courageous, determined and self-assured. What a feeling![3]

## Personal Development

Personal development "covers activities that improve awareness and identity, develop talents and potential, build human capital and facilitate employability, enhance the quality of life and contribute to the realization of dreams and aspirations," according to Wikipedia.[4] For our purposes, personal development represents opportunities that may not be on your radar—at least not when it comes to advancing your career. But these chances to grow, though they may not be directly related to your current position or area of expertise, are still very important to consider. For example, you may know that you're not as strong a speaker as you'd like to be. Committing to joining a speakers group can be an opportunity to gain more self-confidence and prepare you for making your voice and your perspective known in your organization. The same thing is true for learning another language, if that is something you're interested in. You'll flex your learning muscles, gain more confidence in your ability to communicate in other languages, and maybe add a key skill to your résumé that will pay off down the road.

## A Shift in Mindset

A shift in mindset refers to your willingness to experiment with new ways of thinking about—and going about—your work each day, along with new ways of considering your role as an information professional. It includes the ability to shift your focus from doing the same tasks each day in exactly the same manner to gaining a different perspective on that work.

Here's another take on shifting your mindset. You may have noticed a new buzzword popping up everywhere: *pivot*. CEO Jeff Immelt used it to describe how he remade GE.[5] The *Financial Times* devotes a significant amount of space online to discussing *pivot* as it applies to entrepreneurs.[6] It's also a theme in recent career/business books such as *Pivot: The Art and Science of Reinventing Your Career and Life* by Adam Markel. All references to "pivoting" focus on taking action. Markel defines *pivot* as "a small change in direction that creates the potential for transformation."[7]

That act of "pivoting" helps you shift your mindset to leverage all the changes we've been looking at so far. It's the willingness to consider small changes in direction that can add to your career satisfaction and career growth. Notice that Markel uses the words *potential* and *transformation*—two key words that align with the pursuit of growth opportunities. *Potential*, when used to describe the benefits of pursuing opportunities, suggests your ability to shift your mindset and, as a result, take some actions that may result in an outcome (though unknown in the moment) that can boost your career. The "transformation" that Markel mentions also says something about growth opportunities. I'm not talking about overnight magic here, but I am suggesting that the practice of pursuing the right opportunities as a long-term strategy will indeed transform your career into one that is rich with meaning and full of possibilities for ongoing growth.

Pivoting doesn't mean you need to change jobs, relocate, or grab on to just any opportunity to grow your career. The change in direction may be as simple as opening your mind to considering opportunities that will take you deeper or wider in your work. It may mean being willing to take a small (appropriate) risk outside your comfort zone to try something or learn something new. It is action focused—meaning it calls for some action on your part to make it happen. It may mean taking an action that is observable to others. Or it may mean a change in how you think about or approach something.

Growth opportunities are *not* about fulfilling objectives on a yearly performance review—they are bigger than that. They are not a series of random commitments you make without giving any thought as to why you're doing them—or whether they are the best opportunities for you. And they are not activities you sign up for simply because your friends or coworkers are signing up for them too (unless they fall in line with well–thought out plans you've developed for yourself).

Growth opportunities are your surest path to growing your career. Each time you choose to pursue a growth activity, you are building momentum along with your skill set, confidence, and savvy in your field.

## What's in It for You?

Why should you consider pursuing growth opportunities and make it a long-term strategy in your new "workplace smarts" toolbox? First, because it's quite likely that you're reading this book right now because you *are* interested in growing your career and learning more about the opportunities that will keep you engaged and keep your work life meaningful and satisfying.

Still, you might be imagining a number of "yes, but . . ." hesitancies. As in "yes, but . . . pursuing career-growth opportunities will require more work on my part, and I'm already pretty busy." Or "yes, but . . . I'm not sure where to start or whether it will pay off or not." (Feel free to insert your own "yes, but . . ." thinking here.) We all have those moments when taking care of our careers can seem daunting. But the guidelines that follow over the next chapters will clarify the steps you can take to change the process from daunting to do-able. Let's look at some key reasons the practice of pursuing growth opportunities is right for you.

## Five Excellent Reasons for Pursuing Career-Growth Opportunities

If you are experiencing some doubts—or even if you're not, but you'd like to see some smart reasons to pursue growth opportunities—consider these:

*1. Because you want to be seen and valued as a professional—not an amateur.*

Stop for a minute here and reflect back on the reasons you went into librarianship or information services in the first place. Some say it was a "calling" for them. Others say the work fascinated them, or they felt particularly interested in the notion of being able to "organize" information and share it with others. Some people mention the outreach and literacy aspects of the profession. Your reasons may be similar—or not. But I bet that you, like many library and information professionals I have talked with, will mention the desire to gain the specialized skills that the field has to offer. If you're like most LIS workers, you didn't decide to go into this work on a whim. And it's likely you take your work seriously. That marks you as a professional—you are among those who wish to excel in their field—often through taking advantage of growth opportunities that add to your portfolio.

Farnam Street, a thought- and idea-provoking website, notes the differences between professionals and amateurs. I've included some selected key differences here. Notice how each quality of professionalism suggests some aspect of pursuing growth opportunities.

- Amateurs stop when they achieve something. Professionals understand that the initial achievement is just the beginning.
- Amateurs give up at the first sign of trouble and assume they're failures. Professionals see failure as part of the path to growth and mastery.
- Amateurs focus on the short term. Professionals focus on the long term.
- Amateurs go faster. Professionals go further.[8]

*2. Because showing up is not enough—not for your employer and probably not for you either.*

It used to be that "showing up" was enough to guarantee your employment. No more. The truth is, most professionals want to be challenged, contribute value, and make a difference. Seth Godin says it so well: "There are fewer and fewer good jobs where you can get paid merely for showing up. Instead, successful organizations are paying for people who make a difference and are shedding everyone else."[9] Speaking of making a difference, see the next item.

### 3. Because you do want to make a difference.

My guess is, you do want to make a difference; otherwise, you wouldn't have entered your field. But to continue to do so, you will want to make sure you're sharing the latest and most relevant and accurate information. You'll want to be able to explain and demonstrate the most useful technologies. You'll want your outreach efforts to be the most effective. To do these things, your own knowledge and skills cannot remain static. Here's more wisdom from Godin: "What does it mean to make a difference? . . . the really good jobs are going to be filled with indispensable people, people who make a difference by doing work that's really hard to find from anyone else."[10]

### 4. Because it's to your advantage to be on the cutting edge.

As a professional, you can't rely on just what you learned in school or what you've been doing for the past five years. The world is moving too fast for that. Right now, the challenge to be on the cutting edge seems almost impossible. Yet knowing *where* you want to move toward that edge—in *what areas*, serving *what populations*, choosing which *specializations*, or understanding which *technologies*—will be necessary if you want to move forward and not get paralyzed by too many possibilities. That is what choosing and pursuing the right opportunities will let you do. Godin's wisdom works here too. "Raising the bar is easier than it looks, and it pays for itself. If your boss won't raise your bar, you should."[11]

### 5. Because it's important to widen—not narrow—your experience and perspective.

There is some very good news about getting really good at the one area in which you spend most of your work time. You gain expertise in that area—and that makes you the "go-to" person in that specialty niche. But there is also some not-so-good news if you just stick with one particular area and go no further. You might narrow your range of skills and tend to limit your view—or your viewpoint. Writer Ron Carucci conducted an interesting interview with Dorie Clark, author of the recent book *Entrepreneurial You*. In the interview, Clark points out the caution of sticking to a narrow range of skills: "The natural byproduct of doing one job well over time is that your world view actually narrows. You become biased to view things through the lens of your work."[12] So while you're developing expertise in one area, you would be wise to stretch your perspective through identifying opportunities that offer a wider scope (and skill set) as well.

## Four Red Flags If You Choose Not to Pursue Growth Opportunities

If you're looking for further proof that it's in your best interests to consider pursuing growth opportunities, then it's a good idea to look at some possible consequences if you don't. Here are four to consider. Ask yourself if any of these potential stumbling blocks might get in your way and keep you from growing.

### 1. *The danger of educated incapacity*

It's important to strike a balance between being rightfully proud of what you know and presuming that you know just about all there is to know in your field or specialization. We've all worked with individuals who turn down opportunities to try a new technology or resist the chance to take a course on some new approach to getting work done. These individuals say they already have that technology mastered—or that a new approach won't teach them anything they don't already know. But such overconfidence can cost them. Turning down new opportunities may demonstrate an overconfidence that isn't helpful and may get in the way. Herman Kahn at the Hudson Institute refers to this as educated incapacity. He explains it this way: "Educated incapacity often refers to an *acquired or learned inability to understand or even perceive a problem,* much less a solution." Kahn goes on to say that "the more expert . . . a person is, the less likely that person is to see a solution when it is not within the framework in which he or she was taught to think."[13] So having expertise is good. Boasting about—and believing—that you are *the* expert: not so good. If you cannot identify a problem when it comes up, or if you're oblivious to gaps in your own knowledge, then you jeopardize your ability to respond appropriately when circumstances require you to do so.

### 2. *The perils of the Doom Loop*

Back in the late 1970s, Charles Jett created a model to help people make sound, tactical decisions about their careers. He called his model the Doom Loop, though he admits that it isn't so much a loop as it is a catchy name! But don't be fooled by its simplicity. Though the origins of his model are almost forty years old, it is just as relevant and useful today. In fact, in 2015, he wrote *The DOOM LOOP!* to reintroduce it to those in the midst of career quandaries.[14] The Doom Loop, in Jett's model, is a 2 × 2 matrix that includes just two variables: preference (like/don't like) and performance (good at/not good at). Read on to see why Jett's Doom Loop idea fits so well with the benefits of choosing to pursue growth opportunities and the consequences of choosing *not* to pursue them.

As you can see from the matrix on page 36, Jett's Doom Loop matrix has four quadrants. Imagine that quadrant 1 (the lower left) represents the time when someone (like yourself) took on that first professional role. If you can recall what it's like when

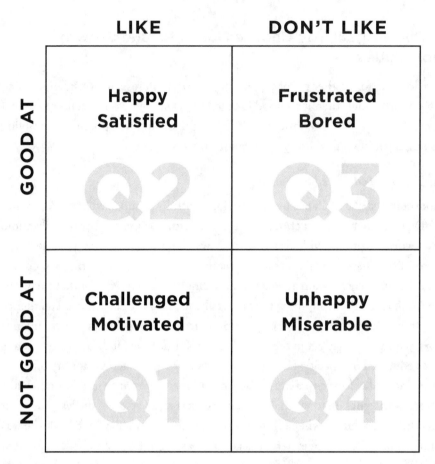

|  | LIKE | DON'T LIKE |
|---|---|---|
| **GOOD AT** | Happy<br>Satisfied<br><br>Q2 | Frustrated<br>Bored<br><br>Q3 |
| **NOT GOOD AT** | Challenged<br>Motivated<br><br>Q1 | Unhappy<br>Miserable<br><br>Q4 |

**Figure 3.1.** Doom Loop matrix

"The Doom Loop" is reprinted with permission from *The DOOM LOOP!* by Charles Cranston Jett (Denver, CO: Outskirts Press, 2015).

you first take on a new position, you can get a picture of what the learning curve is like when you are brand new at something. Think for a moment about what that first week was like for you when you took on your first (or most recent) professional position. For most of us, it's an exciting time because there are so many new learning opportunities ahead; but it's also a time filled with some anxiety, as we begin to grasp just how much there is to learn. In quadrant 1, you're like a sponge—trying to absorb all you can so you can do your very best at your job. Now imagine that about six months have passed and you've moved on to quadrant 2, the point at which you "sort of" know your way around and aren't so overwhelmed by every task you set out to accomplish. Though the learning curve isn't quite so steep, you're still pretty much the new kid on the block. The good news about quadrant 2 is that you're getting better at your job because you have mastered a lot of what it takes to succeed at this point, and you're feeling pretty good about it. Still, you find yourself challenged to continue learning and understand what it takes to succeed in your role. Now imagine it's a year or two later (though times here can vary quite a bit), and you've moved over to quadrant 3, where you feel much more on top of your game, with a pretty solid mastery of your work and a sense of "knowing how things get done around here." But the excitement about all the new things to learn has lost its power. Your attitude in quadrant 3 can take a couple different directions: You can grow complacent, even a bit bored, perhaps, as you begin to take your position, your knowledge, and your abilities for granted. Or you can accept the fact that, though you know a great deal, you must keep learning and growing for the sake of your performance and to stay engaged with your work. In this last scenario, you don't grow complacent or overly self-confident about your abilities.

What do you think the consequences are for these two different types of thinking? As Jett suggests in his book, if you take the "I-know-it-all" route and assume you've arrived, chances are good you're headed into the Doom Loop (quadrant 4), meaning you're doomed by your own complacency. You're a bit less challenged and, therefore, don't push yourself to learn things that will keep you relevant. You may not perform at the level you once did when everything was new—and you may end up with a performance review that is less than stellar. What do you do to stop that Doom Loop from kicking in? You stay fresh and excited about pursuing growth opportunities that will keep you at the top of your game and still give 100 percent to your efforts. The choice is yours.

### 3. The road blocks of limiting beliefs

Limiting beliefs get in our way. Limiting beliefs are the ones that we hang on to, put our faith in—*believe* in—though they don't usually reflect reality. It's just that we have come to believe them—sometimes early in life, for all sorts of reasons—and they tend to shape decisions we make as we go through life, often in a negative way. For example, some people may say "I'm not smart enough" or "I'm not skilled enough" (though there is no proof that such beliefs are true). People who hold on to these limiting beliefs end up giving in to them rather than challenging them. Such limiting beliefs constrain our choices and our actions, and they can keep us from taking on a growth opportunity—if we mistakenly believe we can't handle it. So it's worth your time to pay attention to how you may be stopping yourself from taking any sort of action because of some negative (and untested) message you're giving yourself about what you can and cannot do.

### 4. The challenge of the "thin file"

I came across this term for the first time while reading Iris Bohnet's article in the *New York Times* about this potential promotion roadblock.[15] Bohnet, a behavioral economist, learned of it while researching the challenge faced by women and minorities who were not seen as promotable because they didn't seem to "have what it takes" in terms of a track record of accomplishments achieved through taking on key assignments. Bohnet's findings suggest that individuals with "thin files" had been given fewer opportunities and less feedback to help them improve. I include this thin file dilemma here—not to emphasize possible bias, though that may have been the focus in Bohnet's article, but to highlight the need to practice the YoYo model of career self-management. You may recall from chapter 2 that YoYo stands for "You're on Your own."

If you do not have a portfolio that includes key assignments, accomplishments, or activities, then it is up to you to find and pursue those opportunities yourself. Perhaps your boss cannot afford to let you go to national conferences, or maybe your library system is so small that there are limited opportunities for organization-sponsored professional development. That doesn't mean you can't find venues that you *can* attend on your own—perhaps a regional event closer to home or participation in an online group with other professionals who work in your specialization or area of interest.

Whatever your situation, focus on building a "thicker file"—one that includes participation in the *right* opportunities for you.

## What Employers Think of Growth Opportunities

One of the urgent priorities that organizations are paying attention to right now is talent—as in talent development, talent retention, and talent pipeline. You get it: all things talent-related. And just who or what is the "talent" that organizations are focusing on? YOU! You (if you're doing your part) represent the skills, knowledge, and know-how that organizations so badly need to continue growing and thriving themselves. That's just as true for a nonprofit as it is for a Fortune 500 company. With hypercompetition, a global economy, boomers retiring, and the speed of just about everything accelerating, organizations need to have an edge—and that edge is their awesome employees who contribute their best efforts. And organizations know quite well that to keep their employees on the cutting edge, they need to continually help them upgrade their skills, have the latest knowledge at their fingertips, and give 110 percent. What does that mean, bottom line? It means that smart organizations will partner with those they hire to make certain they have what they need to succeed. It does no good for an organization to hire you because you are at the top of your game and outshine other candidates—only to keep you from staying so smart and adding value. Organizations know that it is in their best interests to help you keep up to speed through supporting you as you pursue growth opportunities.

Yes, there are organizations with tight budgets and others that are running with a rather lean staff. So it's understandable that they don't always have the dollars to send you to every conference, workshop, or seminar that you want to attend. At times, a staff shortage issue may keep you from pursuing the kind of additional training or growth experience you believe you need. That doesn't mean you can't keep growing. Most workplaces do not want you walking out the door and moving on to some other organization that will benefit from your talent. The title of a book by Beverly Kaye and Julie Giulioni states the issue pretty clearly: *Help Them Grow or Watch Them Go.*[16]

And before you point out that not every organization is so enlightened, I agree. But the old debate about who has responsibility for your continued growth—you or your employer—has, for the most part, shifted to a conversation about how an employer and its employees can share that responsibility and who should be providing what. These days, it's more likely that an employer is expected to provide ways (resources, training, support, mentoring, coaching) to help you continue to grow, and you are expected to step up with the commitment and follow through to ensure your value and contribution to the organization that has hired you. Organizations and workers alike are still figuring out the best way to share this responsibility. Review the "Career Conversations" section in chapter 8 for ideas on how to talk with your manager or supervisor about this issue.

When it comes to growth opportunities that you want to pursue, some will cost money, and others will require time away from your day-to-day responsibilities. Some that are organization-based may require the approval of one or more people you report to. For these, it will be good to have a strategy in mind for making the case to your manager for how this growth opportunity will also benefit your organization. But there are also several other types of growth opportunities that you can initiate on your own, and many that don't require someone else's approval or budget. Stay tuned—we're covering a wide range of these in chapter 7.

Beyond the several good reasons to pursue growth opportunities mentioned earlier—along with the possible consequences if you don't—it's critical for you to understand what you'll need to grow your career from here. First, let's look at what will be required of you to take full advantage of growth opportunities.

## What You'll Need to Bring to the Table

If you want to make the most of pursuing growth opportunities, great! But *just wanting to* isn't enough. Read through the items that follow to see the attitudes and actions that will best position you to pursue and make the most of whatever growth opportunities you choose.

### Deep Knowledge of Yourself

This requirement goes much deeper than the self-assessment you did back in school or even the one you did prior to taking on your current position. If you're not currently employed, it's just as important. If you don't know who you are, then you can't possibly know which opportunities are right for you to pursue. Chapter 4 will give you the tools you'll need to gain this deep knowledge of yourself.

## Growth Mindset

The word *mindset* seems almost overused at the moment. We read about an optimistic mindset, a spiritual mindset, or a team-oriented mindset. And in many cases, you may be thinking, *What's the big deal with mindset, anyway?* It *is* a big deal because it sets the stage for your success. The right mindset prepares you mentally—it gets you excited to begin. *Mindset,* according to Dictionary.com, refers to "an attitude, disposition, or mood, an intention or inclination."[17] In other words, *mindset* refers to our attitudes and the general ways we approach our lives and our work. The idea of *mindset* is important here because how you approach your work and your career future has a lot to do with your attitudes and how you think about your possibilities for your career going forward.

A *growth* mindset is the focus of this section. Such a mindset is extremely important because it sets everything in motion. It builds momentum. It motivates. It "creates a passion for learning," which can then lead to more opportunities.[18] For our purposes in this book, I am using Carol Dweck's description of a growth mindset, which she notes

> is based on the belief that your basic qualities are things you can cultivate through your efforts. Although people may differ in every which way—in their initial talents and aptitudes, interests, or temperaments—everyone can change and grow through application and experience.[19]

Dr. Dweck goes on to say that people with a growth mindset "believe that a person's true potential is unknown (and unknowable); that it's impossible to foresee what can be accomplished with years of passion, toil, and training."[20] Can you see how, if you believe that you can change your circumstances, learn something new, benefit from the pursuit of some new learning, or increase your expertise, you can shape your career going forward?

## Über Adaptability

Über has become common in our everyday conversations whenever we want to convey the idea that something is "over the top." I use it here to emphasize that it's not simply being adaptable that will do it for you in our current workplaces. Your adaptability needs to go "over the top" as well.

According to *Oxford Dictionary*, über means "to a great or extreme degree and denoting an outstanding or supreme example of a particular kind of person or thing."[21] And *Merriam-Webster* defines über as "being a superlative example of its kind or class."[22] Both sources suggest that über-anything means that particular "thing," person, or quality stands out. That's exactly what's required of you in this item.

Adaptable means "able to adjust to new conditions," per *Oxford Dictionary*.[23] When it comes to career adaptability, "companies need employees who are open to new ideas, flexible enough to work through challenging issues and generally able to cope when things don't go as planned," according to an article on Chron.com.[24]

The ante has been upped if you want to pursue and succeed at growth opportunities. A shorthand version of this über adaptability I'm talking about would be the ability to turn on a dime without missing a beat—and to be able to remain focused, committed, and engaged the whole time. Sounds a bit like the description for Superman or Superwoman, doesn't it?

The use of both words together suggests that the stakes have been raised. Being "adaptable" or "flexible" have long been the hallmarks of traits suggested as critical to the new world of work. But the long-held notion that a worker is adaptable if she can accommodate new changes, or if he can modify his way of going about a task when it's necessary to do so, simply isn't enough in the emerging workplace. Today's professionals must actually embody the "über adaptability" I'm referring to here—they must breathe it, believe in it, and demonstrate it.

## Double Vision

Double vision is the need for a future focus coupled with a clear view of what's happening around you in the present. Spotting growth opportunities means you need to be hyperaware of what is going on in your workplace (or in the one you hope to join), in your field, and in your area of specialization, if you have one. For example: What are the hot issues? The exciting new developments? The worrisome areas that may be cut back? The mission and strategic plan for this coming year? If you don't know what is going on around you, then how can you know where you might contribute?

Likewise, it's imperative for you to know what's on the horizon—the people and issues that will soon be part of your field, your workplace, or the work you do. There are several ways to be "in the know" when it comes to the future. Reading magazines and journals from your field is a requirement. But also consider reading outside your field, attending events that are complementary to your field—and even ones that aren't. If you're into community engagement, for instance, there are a number of venues where you can become more knowledgeable about this topic—and you can bring this information back to your home workplace where you can leverage and share what you know. Another great place is through acquainting yourself with future trends—especially those that will impact your field. Be sure to check out the latest trends discussed in chapter 5.

## Curiosity

Think for a moment about why you chose to become a library or information professional. My guess is that curiosity was one of your motivators. And your ongoing fascination with *what if*, *why*, and *how* questions is what makes you so helpful to a student, a client, or a patron with puzzling, hard-to-answer queries.

Take Bretagne Byrd, bookmobile librarian for Lewis & Clark Library in Helena, Montana, for example. In a recent interview, Bretagne shared with me a challenge she had in wanting to serve the kids she interacted with on her bookmobile stops. Her main library had 3-D printers, and Bretagne really wanted to take this technology out on the road with her. After some research, Bretagne discovered 3-D pens that she could pack up in her bookmobile and share with kids on her trips. Together, they were able to make dinosaurs, planters, glasses, and even the Eiffel Tower! Obviously, this was a big hit for the children who visited the bookmobile—and they got to experience a new technology because Bretagne was curious about how she could make this happen.[25]

Curiosity has a magic of its own, as Jillian Reilly notes: "We forget that the magic of learning resides in that delicious space of NOT knowing—that we grow the most when we embrace the unknown. As adults, we forget that questions, not answers, are the key to our success."[26] This same curiosity will lead you to explore opportunities that may not be obvious or easy to track down at first.

## Insatiable Appetite for Learning

This particular quality may have been another one of the factors that drew you to librarianship in the first place. There's a bit of a buzz to learning about those things worth knowing. To uncover growth opportunities, you need to be willing to do your homework, research new possibilities, and learn how they might apply to you. Your voracious hunger for learning has other benefits too. It is often a mark of learning agility—a highly prized attribute in today's workplace.

Monique Valcour, writing in *Harvard Business Review*, describes it this way:

> Learning agility is the capacity for rapid, continuous learning from experience. Agile learners are good at making connections across experiences, and they're able to let go of perspectives or approaches that are no longer useful—in other words, they can unlearn things when novel solutions are required. People with this mindset tend to be oriented toward learning goals and open to new experiences. . . . A desire

to develop by acquiring new skills and mastering new situations is a fundamental element of learning agility. Agile learners value and derive satisfaction from the process of learning itself which boosts their motivation as well as their capacity to learn from challenging developmental experiences.[27]

Learning about new opportunities will allow you to continue to take your learning further and make it a part of your long-term growth plan.

## Initiative

Sure, you've probably heard at least a couple dozen times throughout your career that "taking initiative" is the way to move ahead. And though the advice is true, you still need to decide just how and when you want to make initiative a strategy for you. It is definitely to your advantage to use initiative to go after growth opportunities. I promise you they won't show up in your e-mails each morning with a catchy subject line like "Open now for an incredible growth opportunity that's been chosen for you!" It's possible—but not very likely. As is true in all other areas of YoYo Land, you have to step up.

But you can calibrate your decision to take initiative—you don't have to go for the biggest challenge you can think of. Instead, you can heed the advice given in Gregg Levoy's book, *Callings*.[28] Think of taking initiative as you would think of taking a do-able risk: "One step further than where you are right now."

It's the stepping up that matters. Others notice when you do it. Even if it's for a task that others on your committee aren't willing to take on—if it's one that gives you a bit more knowledge, skills, or the chance to network, do it. Here's another gem of wisdom from Seth Godin on the topic of initiative. And he's spot-on with his observation. "A job is not enough. A factory is not enough. A trade is not enough. It used to be, but no longer. The world is changing too fast. Without the spark of initiative, you have no choice but to simply react to the world. Without the ability to instigate and experiment, you are stuck, adrift, waiting to be shoved."[29]

## Perseverance

Most of us are familiar with this one. Think back to what it took to finish your studies, get that job, or complete that long-term assignment that seemed to be filled with every possible obstacle. That's perseverance. We know it as simply hanging in there when we would rather not. Perseverance, that ability to continue our best efforts in spite of the challenges, is a requirement for succeeding at the growth opportunities you pursue. Since many of these pursuits will be self-initiated, done with or without the support of others, you must find a way to stay motivated to complete what you started.

## Change-ability

By change-ability, I'm referring to your ability to flow with changes as they come your way. I'm also referring to what Antoine Tirard and Claire Harbour-Lyell describe as *change agility*. Here is how they describe it:

> Change agility is your natural level of comfort in new or unsettling situations. Some people are more tolerant of uncertainty and can handle it well. Valuing new perspectives and viewing problems as opportunities will increase your creativity, resourcefulness and self-confidence.[30]

When I think of change-ability, I think of my nephew, Ryan. Ryan, together with a group of friends, decided to visit Thailand. It would be the first time out of the States for each person in the group. As it got closer to their departure date, one by one, Ryan's friends determined that they couldn't make the trip. Undaunted (and change-able), Ryan decided he'd go alone and make the most of his solo adventure. And he did just that. He could have let go of the idea of going on the trip since he'd have to go alone, but he didn't. Ryan's attitude in this instance was just a part of his overall willingness to take risks and be open to changes as they came his way.

Take a moment now and reflect on your own feelings about change. Do you look ahead with trepidation, worrying about what the latest workplace changes might mean for you? Do you prefer to keep up the routine of the known, the familiar, for as long as possible? Or do you look forward to the new, the different, as a chance to learn something you didn't know before?

I realize that for some of you, becoming more change-able isn't the issue—boredom is. You're secretly wishing that you *could* have the chance to demonstrate that you are change-able.

For people I talk with who describe themselves as bored or stuck, *their* struggle is to stay engaged. So let's take a look at boredom and how pursuing growth opportunities may help.

When we're faced with an issue in our careers that is uncomfortable and unwanted, like feeling bored or stuck, it can be very frustrating. At that moment, it's difficult to see that situations *do* shift over time, and while we're in the middle of our boredom or "stuckness," it's likely that we may get a bit anxious because we feel helpless to change our situation at that moment. When we're anxious, our vision narrows, our options seem to diminish, and our world gets smaller. That's only natural—we move into a kind of survival mode or holding pattern. And usually, when this happens, our problem-solving skills go out the window, along with our ability to see a future that is any different.

But what if you *could* do something different in those moments when you feel bored or stuck? Rather than just keeping your head down or your eyes closed, what if you took the courageous step of exploring what else is possible? I promise you that if you're willing to give this last option a try, you are likely to see the boredom lift, the stress that comes with change diminish, and the opportunity to stretch and expand appear. You'll see your options increase rather than decrease. So the next time you're feeling a bit stuck or bored, take a breath, ease back, and ask yourself this: *What kind of opportunity might shift my perspective or my possibilities for change right now?*

## Notes

1. Dictionary.com, "Opportunity," www.dictionary.com/browse/opportunity?s=t.
2. Oxford Dictionaries, "Professional Development," https://en.oxforddictionaries.com/definition/professional_development/.
3. Beatrice Calvin, phone interview with the author, January 19, 2018.
4. Wikipedia.org, "Personal Development," https://en.wikipedia.org/wiki/Personal_development/.
5. Jeffrey R. Immelt, "How I Remade GE and What I Learned along the Way," *Harvard Business Review*, August 24, 2017, www.alumni.hbs.edu/stories/Pages/story-bulletin.aspx?num=6377/.
6. *Financial Times*, "Pivot," http://lexicon.ft.com/Term?term=pivot/.
7. Steve Farber, "Six Critical Steps You Must Take Before Every Big Decision." *Inc.*, March 9, 2018, www.inc.com/steve-farber/6-critical-steps-you-must-take-before-every-big-decision.html.
8. Farnam Street, "The Difference between Amateurs and Professionals," n.d., www.fs.blog/2017/08/amateurs-professionals/.
9. Seth Godin, *Linchpin: Are You Indispensable?* (New York: Penguin Group, 2010), 23.
10. Ibid.
11. Ibid, 70.
12. Ron Carucci, "Why Everyone Needs a Portfolio Career," *Forbes*, September 25, 2017, www.forbes.com/sites/roncarucci/2017/09/25/three-reasons-everyone-needs-a-portfolio-career/#59ec4b5e4d07/.
13. Herman Kahn, "The Expert and Educated Incapacity," Hudson Institute, June 1, 1979. www.hudson.org/research/2219-the-expert-and-educated-incapacity/.
14. Charles Cranston Jett, *The Doom Loop! Straight Talk about Job Frustration, Boredom, Career Crises and Tactical Career Decisions from the Doom Loop Creator* (Denver, CO: Outskirts Press, 2015).
15. Iris Bohnet, "Tackling 'The Thin File' That Can Prevent a Promotion," *New York Times*, October 3, 2017, www.nytimes.com/2017/10/03/business/women-minority-promotion.html.
16. Beverly Kaye and Julie Giulioni, *Help Them Grow or Watch Them Go: Career Conversations Employees Want* (San Francisco: Berrett-Koehler, 2012).
17. Dictionary.com, "Mind-set," www.dictionary.com/browse/mindset?s=t/.
18. Carol S. Dweck, *Mindset: The New Psychology of Success* (New York: Ballantine Books, 2006), 7.
19. Ibid.
20. Ibid.
21. Oxford Dictionaries, "Definition of Uber," https://en.oxforddictionaries.com/definition/uber-.
22. Merriam-Webster, "Über-," www.merriam-webster.com/dictionary/über-/.
23. Oxford Dictionary, "Adaptable," https://en.oxforddictionaries.com/definition/adaptable/.
24. Neil Kokemuller, "How to Demonstrate Adaptability on the Job," Chron, http://work.chron.com/demonstrate-adaptability-job-15407.html.

25. Bretagne Byrd, phone interview with the author, November 2, 2017.

26. Jillian Reilly, "#1 Most Under-Rated Leadership Skill: Are You Curious?," Braveshift, September 26, 2017, https://braveshift.com/are-you-curious/.

27. Monique Valcour, "4 Ways to Be a Better Learner," *Harvard Business Review*, December 31, 2015. https://www.hbrascend.in/topics/4-ways-to-become-a-better-learner/.

28. Gregg Michael Levoy, *Callings: Finding and Following an Authentic Life* (New York: Crown, 1998).

29. Seth Godin, *Poke the Box: When Was the Last Time You Did Something for the First Time?* (New York: Portfolio, 2015), 4.

30. Antoine Tirard and Claire-Harbour-Lyell, "The Mindset That Fosters Agility," INSEAD, August 14, 2017, https://knowledge.insead.edu/node/6891/pdf.

## CHAPTER 4

· · · · · · · · · ·

# How Well Do You Know *You?*

W arning! Skip this chapter at your own risk—and at the risk of your career future.

I begin with this warning because I believe that knowing yourself is *that* important. Some people, when they see anything related to self-assessment, automatically switch into "been there, done that" mode and skip ahead in whatever they're reading. But just because you did some self-assessment in school, as part of a performance appraisal, or in some team-building exercise doesn't mean you know as much as you need to know and understand about yourself to go forward and take on growth opportunities. As writer Erin Palmer puts it, "You can't better yourself and get what you want from work until you know yourself."[1] While you may be able to easily rattle off the names of a dozen assessments you've taken over the life of your academic studies and your career, I hope you'll stick with this chapter before you launch into going after growth opportunities. I promise—it will be painless (though it will take some time and focused attention on your part)—and it will give you the foundation you need to go forward.

You may find that to answer some of the questions in this chapter and the next one, you'll need to dig a little deeper or do a bit of research inside the organization you work for—or through hunting up some data online. Consider the ALA (www.ala. org), Library Journal (lj.libraryjournal.com), and the website for the institution and program where you completed your LIS-related academic training, as well as the website for any other library or information service–related associations you may belong to that reflect your particular area of work (such as the Public Library Association [www.ala.org/pla/], Special Libraries Association [www.sla.org/], or other relevant groups). All these sites have important information about positions in the field, information about the tasks of library staff members in specific job titles found within job announcements, information on the job outlook for library and information-related positions in general, and library and information-related trends for the future. You'll find these sites to be a gold mine when you want to learn more about the full range of growth opportunities across the LIS spectrum.

Still with me? Good! Let's get to it.

Peter Drucker was right. Drucker, one of the top business gurus of all time, wrote an article that became a classic some years back (and it's still relevant today), making the case for "managing oneself." By that, he meant that accurately assessing/knowing yourself must come before anything else.[2] Why? Think of it this way: If you don't know what's important to you, how will you know which direction to go? If you don't know what your strengths are (in detail, not just the broad strokes), how can you demonstrate them, leverage them, or even know what to do with them to advance yourself? And how will you be able to identify growth opportunities that build on your key strengths? If you don't know your most marketable, important, relevant, and valued skills, how can you offer them to anybody who is looking for what you have to offer—not just to hire you, but to consider you for *any* opportunities? If you don't know what you value, how will you know what's important to you and critical in choosing the right opportunities to pursue? You get the picture—without an accurate self-appraisal, you might as well blindfold yourself, grab a dart, try to aim for the dartboard (that you can't see since you are now blindfolded), and hope you hit the target—or even come anywhere close.

## Self-Knowledge + Growth Opportunities = Unlimited Career Possibilities

Assessments that are designed to gauge skills, interests, strengths, weaknesses, aptitudes, abilities, and similar qualities are most often completed when you're trying to choose a college major or career, when you've applied for a job and your prospective employer wants to know more about you than what's on your résumé, when it's time for a performance appraisal, and sometimes when you're up for a promotion.

There is usually a somewhat standard array of qualifications/qualities that are assessed: skills, knowledge, abilities, personality traits, team membership qualities, leadership potential, values, and maybe some other specific measures that relate to your area of expertise. Taken together, these assessments are meant to give your college advisor, career coach, manager, or the organization that is screening you for a job or a promotion a solid picture of you—what you can bring to the table, how you would perform as part of a team, your knowledge when it comes to your particular specialty, as well as your potential weaknesses, and areas for further development. Pretty straightforward.

But when it comes to identifying and going after growth opportunities, the results of any self-assessment are pure gold *for you!* They don't need to be passed on to a supervisor for evaluation or approval, and they don't need to be analyzed to send you off toward the right career. Self-appraisal, when done to help select the best growth opportunities, is there for you to use on your own behalf. If you get a clear picture of who you are right now—including the facets that make you unique, your view of your future, your passions, what you want to contribute, how you want to make a difference, and what curiosities and concerns you have about your field—you have a recipe for moving your career forward that is brilliant and full of options! (*I realize I get a bit overexcited about this topic at times!*)

## Reflect First

Before you dive into the self-assessment section in this chapter, it's a good idea to begin reflecting on the areas that are essential to your having a deep and comprehensive understanding of yourself. To help you do that, I've listed a series of questions for you to thoughtfully consider. Once you have reviewed these questions and how you might respond to them, move on to the self-assessment section. The time and effort you put into both sections will definitely pay off when you choose the best growth opportunities for you to pursue.

First, some warm-up questions to get you thinking: you can simply reflect on these or jot down some notes if that helps you begin to clarify your thinking.

1. Do you know your five top skills—the ones you're most competent in—and how you got so good at them?
2. What are one or two skills you're good at but wish you'd never have to use again?
3. Why wouldn't you want to use them?
4. Which skills would you like to use more of if you had the opportunity to do so?
5. If you could get really good at something that has nothing to do with your current job or area of specialization, what would it be? Why?
6. What knowledge do you possess that would make you a smart hire?
7. What five values are most important to you?
8. In what ways do you think you make a difference in your job—or, how would you *like* to make a difference in the job you aspire to?
9. Professionally speaking, what absolutely fascinates you?
10. List the highlights of what you've learned that's new over the last year.
11. What are your top three strengths and how are you using them right now? (*Consider strengths the things you do best at in your work each day.*)
12. How would you like to use them more?
13. Which strengths aren't you using? Why not?

14. If you were a car, what kind of car would you be? Why? (*I had to throw this last question in—makes it a bit more fun and engages your creative side!*)

Many of these questions—or variations of them—show up in a lot of assessments. Yet too often we answer them as though we're on "automatic" without giving serious thought to them. Or we answer them the same way we did five or ten years ago, just out of habit. Or we don't really distinguish between our skills, our knowledge, or our strengths. That makes our results vague, not clearly defined, and not a reflection of who we are now and which direction we want to go as we look forward. Your self-assessment responses include elements of your history—that's how you got where you are! But your assessment responses should also give hints about the future you want to move toward.

## Discover Who You Are Now

Ready to begin your self-assessment? Consider this next section as time well spent—a gift you're giving yourself and the key to maximizing the growth of your career.

To get you off to the best possible start, let's begin with some tried-and-true assessment areas that are worth your focused time and effort. For each area, I'll include some key questions for you to reflect on; hopefully, some of these questions will help you uncover some assets and other important qualities you may not have picked up on in doing other assessments.

The trifecta of self-assessments that most of us are familiar with, when it comes to workplace performance, is often represented by the letters KSA: Knowledge, Skills, and Abilities. KSAs are not simply useful for measuring performance or for determining a person's hiring qualifications (although that is how they're often used). They also can help you get a baseline that you can use to evaluate possible growth opportunities. So let's start with these three areas—once we've covered the traditional ways KSAs have been focused on, I want to take that KSA idea a bit further and suggest you look at other complementary areas that will give you some more important clues about yourself. The next three sections will explain this in more detail.

For definitions and descriptions of knowledge, skills, and abilities, I'm using the words of author F. John Reh because he captures a solid explanation of each area so well.

> **Knowledge** focuses on the actual understanding of particular concepts. It is theoretical and not practical. An individual may have an understanding or textbook knowledge of a topic or tool, but have no experience attempting to apply it or to leverage it as part of his or her job activities.[3]

Here is an example of what knowledge looks like. In your studies, you may have read a text for a course like Applied Research Methods. You may have the *knowledge* and understand the theory behind the subject through your reading, but in most instances, after reading the text, you don't have experience (yet) applying what you learned through your reading.

> **Skills** reflect capabilities or proficiencies developed through training or actual experience. Skills reflect the practical application of the theoretical knowledge.[4]

For example, going back to our first example, you may take knowledge gained in a course on Applied Research Methods (as described on the San Jose State University website, for instance), and through further training or through experience, you should be able to successfully demonstrate basic *skills* of "evaluating, planning, designing, executing, and applying research."[5]

> **Abilities** are those innate capabilities that you bring to a particular task or situation.[6]

Reh, who I cite in this section for his definitions of knowledge, skills, and abilities, offers a great example that illustrates the differences among the three:

> As a negotiator, you can apply your **knowledge** and probing **skills** to help two parties reach a common understanding and agreement on the way forward. While anyone can learn approaches to negotiation and attempt to leverage them, the **ability** of the negotiator to help two parties move from disagreement to agreement transcends the theoretical knowledge and simple skills application.[7]

### Knowledge

With these definitions and examples in mind, let's start your self-assessment process with a focus first on knowledge.

 **Notes to Myself**

**In the space on the next page, write down the knowledge you currently hold, related to aspects of your chosen field.** Specifically, what knowledge do you bring to the table from classes you may have taken as part of your studies, continuing education courses, certificate programs, webinars, or books? Include the knowledge you have that is the most up-to-date, relevant, and valued in the area you currently work in or the area you would like to work in (if you're still a student or not currently employed). Make sure the knowledge you include in the section below is knowledge that you believe you have a pretty good grasp of—not the areas where you know "just a little."

_____

_____

_____

_____

Knowledge, on its own, is of high value. You couldn't apply for a position in your field without it and you couldn't do your job without it either. But it's not enough. Just like everything else in our evolving workplace where expectations keep growing, you need to take it a step further.

As proof of that, take a look at a fascinating view of knowledge offered by author Ian Leslie in his book *Curious*. He introduces readers to the value of possessing both a breadth and a depth of knowledge (another sign that the bar has been raised!). Here is how he puts it:

> In the marketplace for talent, the people most in demand will always be those who offer an expertise few others possess. But having a breadth of knowledge is increasingly valuable, too. These two trends exist in tension with each other. Should you focus on learning more about your own niche or on widening your knowledge base?[8]

Here is Leslie's perspective on that question, in which he compares two types of thinking and recommends a melding of both:

> The thinkers best positioned to thrive today, and in the future, will be a hybrid. . . . In a highly competitive, high-information world, it's crucial to know one or two big things and to know them in more depth and detail than most of your contemporaries. But to really ignite that knowledge, you need the ability to think about it from a variety of eclectic perspectives and to be able to collaborate fruitfully with people who have different specializations.[9]

Leslie gives an example of what such thinking and knowledge would look like by describing what he says is IBM's approach, "T-shaped knowledge":

The most valuable twenty-first century workers combine deep skills in a specialty (the vertical axis of the T) with a broad understanding of other disciplines (the horizontal axis). The former allows them to execute projects that require particular expertise; the latter enables them to see contextual links to other disciplines. Having a core competency differentiates [an individual] in the market place—it gives her a USP (unique selling proposition) within her organization and beyond it—while the top line of the T enables her to constructively link up with colleagues from different fields and to adapt to different challenges throughout her career.[10]

Seth Godin underscores this point and confirms how much the bar has been raised:

Wikipedia and the shared knowledge of the Internet make domain knowledge on its own worth significantly less than it used to be. Today, if all you have to offer is that you know a lot of reference book information, you lose, because the Internet knows more than you do. Depth of knowledge combined with good judgment is worth a lot. Depth of knowledge combined with diagnostic skills or nuanced insight is worth a lot, too.[11]

With this nuanced perspective of knowledge that is both broad and deep, respond to the following question:

What is your own version of "T-shaped knowledge"?

Think about the knowledge you possess and fill in the following graphic:

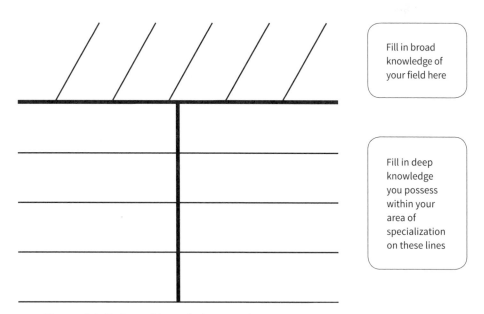

Fill in broad knowledge of your field here

Fill in deep knowledge you possess within your area of specialization on these lines

**Figure 4.1.** T-shaped knowledge exercise

### Know-How

Let's turn next to a cousin of knowledge: *know-how*. As in having the "know-how" to get the job done. It involves a practical understanding of *how* work gets accomplished in a particular workplace, with its unspoken rules and its underlying workplace culture that needs to be acknowledged. Think of the unfortunate (sometimes initially clueless) new worker in an organization who tries to accomplish a task and is told, "That won't work, you need to do it this way." The new worker's response might well be, "That's not the way we did it at my old organization!" And with that reply, the new worker is now viewed as someone who just doesn't "get it" in terms of understanding the new company's culture. Know-how isn't picked up overnight, but it can be learned through observation, asking good questions, and learning how more senior workers manage to successfully run the gauntlet of hidden agendas and homegrown ways to accomplish tricky challenges. We can also think of know-how as "savvy." *Oxford Dictionary* defines *savvy* as "practical knowledge; the ability to make good judgements"[12] Savvy becomes increasingly important for strategizing the growth of your own career.

I want to emphasize that when I use the terms *know-how* or *savvy*, I do not mean how you might get things done by going behind someone else's back or by blatantly ignoring the "rules" inside your organization. Quite the contrary—I mean *know-how* as it relates to being successful in getting things accomplished while playing inside the rules, but with common sense, good judgment, and a keen understanding of the best way forward.

 **Notes to Myself**

What "know-how" do you possess? What would you say you are savvy about when it comes to getting things accomplished (either in your current workplace or in a past position)?

_____

_____

_____

_____

*Skills*

Now that we've covered different aspects of *knowledge* and *know-how*, let's move on to *skills*. Earlier in this chapter, you read a definition of *skills* as "capabilities or proficiencies developed through training or actual experience."[13] You've probably seen discussions of skills that go a bit further—those that distinguish between "hard" skills and "soft" skills. Let's take a moment here to look at both types—because you'll want to consider both (not just one or the other) as you summarize your own list of skills.

According to Alison Doyle, writing on thebalance.com, "soft skills are much more difficult to define and measure—they are the interpersonal or 'people' skills that help you to successfully interact with others in the workplace. Regardless of the job, you have to interact effectively with supervisors and people above and below you on the work chart, as well as others such as customers, vendors, patients, students, etc."[14] So think of all the skills you demonstrate in your interactions with others that help you get your work accomplished. These could include communication, teamwork, listening skills, empathy, problem solving, creativity, adaptability, and critical thinking, among others.

In our current (and future) workplaces, soft skills are edging out hard skills in many instances. As futurist Jennifer Jarratt told me years ago, "the ability to play well with others" continues to increase in importance.[15]

 **Notes to Myself**

**Fill in the spaces below with what you consider to be your top soft skills.** Don't assume that everyone has them because they don't; some people excel in certain ones but not in others. Think for a moment of an individual you may know who may be outstanding in research but just doesn't seem to listen well—and then consider how an inability to listen can be a detriment to that person's work. Others may listen but not be able to take that information into account in making decisions as part of a team. We all have different soft skills in which we excel. Write yours down here:

_____

_____

_____

_____

_____

Now let's turn to the "hard" skills. The definition of these is very similar to the definition of skills in general that was mentioned earlier in this chapter. I'm including an expanded definition of hard skills here so you can compare hard and soft skills. Here's Allison Doyle again, with her definition of hard skills:

> Hard skills are part of the skill set that is required for a job. They include the expertise necessary for an individual to successfully do the job. They are job-specific and are typically listed in job postings and job descriptions. Hard skills are acquired through formal education and training programs, including college, apprenticeships, short-term training classes, online courses, certification programs, as well as by on-the-job training.[16]

Her definition of hard skills acquired through formal educational programs suggests that a person has had the chance to put that formal education to the test—it doesn't stop with simply gaining the knowledge through schooling. Acquired knowledge that's been tested, tried out, practiced, and improved upon is what turns it into skills.

 **Notes to Myself**

**List at least seven of your top "hard" skills.** These skills should be ones that are relevant to your profession and in demand now (not necessarily the ones that were in demand a couple decades ago—unless they are still in demand today). Not sure if the ones you're listing are in demand? Check the latest jobs advertised on a site like ALA's Job List.[17] Or, look at other sites advertising jobs in your specialty. Look for positions that are similar to the job you hold (or ones you've held previously) and read through the qualifications section of the job announcement. Though job requirements vary from one work setting and organization to the next, you'll probably still get a good sense of the current relevancy of your skills.

_____

_____

_____

_____

_____

_____

_____

_____

**Using the skills you've listed above, record those hard skills that represent the skills you truly enjoy using.**

_____

_____

_____

_____

_____

_____

_____

_____

**Finally, record the hard skills you've listed as your top ones that you would be just fine with never using again.**

_____

_____

_____

_____

Here's a piece of wisdom that comes with acknowledging the skills you most enjoy using and the ones you'd rather stop using *right now*! The ones you most enjoy using are generally considered the skills that motivate and excite you—these are the ones you would probably want to do more of. And the ones you'd like to stop using? Those are the ones that likely represent your burnout skills—you may be good at them, but because you don't like using them, it's likely that when you *do* use them, you aren't highly motivated or excited. You just feel burned out! The same is true if your job requires you to do some tasks frequently that you are *not* good at—and probably don't have a desire to be good at. Being asked to use these skills can definitely burn you out or leave you feeling dissatisfied.

### Strengths

Let's take a look at an area that often makes use of your most motivated skills but goes a step further: your *strengths*. Per the career-related website MyWorldofWork.com, "Strengths are things you're naturally good at. If you're good at something, you'll usually find it easier to do. That means you'll feel more confident and engaged, and you'll perform better."[18]

Over the last decade or so, the idea of "strengths" has gained prominence in the workplace. The leading thinkers on strengths, like Tom Rath, author of *StrengthsFinder 2.0*, and Marcus Buckingham, author of *Now, Discover Your Strengths*, have sought to explain the benefits of looking at strengths and how to capitalize on them, rather than spend so much time trying to address weaknesses. Many workplaces too have shifted their emphasis to helping employees identify and use their strengths to greater advantage. To rephrase the words of Tom Rath, strengths are really about doing what one does *best* at work each day.[19] So with that thought in mind, consider what it is that *you* do best each day in your work. Don't worry about trying to figure out if it's a skill, some specialized knowledge you possess, or a particular talent that you exhibit. Simply ask yourself, *What is it that I do really well in my work?* And if you aren't able to do it every day, don't let that stop you from noting it here. Right now, the important point is getting a good sense of the things you do very, very well. You don't have to capture it in one word either. Write down whatever word or phrase seems to capture each strength best.

## ✎ Notes to Myself

**List your top five strengths here, along with a few words detailing how you are using them now—even if it's not every day (or note how you've used them in the past).**

_____

_____

_____

_____

_____

### *Abilities*

To complete the KSA trifecta, let's look at *abilities*. Think of abilities as the particular or unique ways you may have of approaching the task in front of you, or how you go about your work. For instance, every one of your colleagues may be able to answer a reference question, but perhaps you have a way of doing it that makes you especially helpful; or you may be able to "teach" the person asking the question some things that may help him know how to find what he's looking for the next time he needs to do it. Maybe you're great at time management. Or you're especially good at communicating complex ideas. Perhaps you are great under pressure and able to keep a cool head when others are in panic mode.

## Notes to Myself

**List at least five of your abilities here**. If you get stuck, ask some colleagues who know you well for their take on your particular abilities.

_____

_____

_____

_____

_____

### Attitude

In addition to abilities, there is another complementary area worth your attention: **attitude**. According to Dictionary.com, attitude refers to "manner, disposition, feeling, position, etc., with regard to a person or thing."[20]

If you were to try to gauge someone on this "attitude" dimension, it wouldn't be the presence or absence of attitude that you would be noticing—it would be the overall _way_ the person approaches work and workplace-related issues. Does she see the glass as half full or half empty? Does he jump into a tough challenge with the idea of seeing what can be learned and accomplished? Or does he grudgingly (and with a big sigh) move toward the task or issue with a resigned and negative perspective?

Many years ago, psychologist Martin Seligman noted that "how you handle adversity in the workplace tends to have much more impact on your career than how you handle the good stuff."[21] He was right—approaching our career and its challenges with optimism and a positive attitude means that we're more likely to stay with it and not give up. And having an overall sense of optimism and positive attitude has been shown to be of great benefit in giving meaning and offering satisfaction to those who practice it.

Though we may not always be aware of our attitude throughout our workday, it is a critical element in our ability to move forward successfully; and we shouldn't lose sight of that fact. Our attitude shapes our days and our future. In the words of author Jon Acuff, "We—not our company—are responsible for our attitudes. What happens each day at work doesn't get to determine my attitude, I do. Attitude is a decision. And it's a decision we have to make every day."[22]

Given that you can't "measure" your level of positive attitude, it is still worth reflecting on your own half-full versus half-empty approach to life and especially toward your own work and career. Reflect on recent challenges, tasks, or issues you've needed to deal with in your workplace (or, if you're not employed at the moment, consider situations in your daily life that have come up recently) and answer these questions:

## Notes to Myself

**How did you approach the situation? What were you feeling when you considered how to deal with it? How would you describe your attitude at that time?**

_____

_____

_____

How do you think your perspective here might be similar to your perspective on trying new things?

• • •

## Values

A short definition of *values* might include those things, ideals, or beliefs that are most important to us. Why is it essential to determine your values as you consider career-related matters? When we work in alignment with things that matter most to us, we find satisfaction and meaning in what we do. But when we do work that is in conflict with what we value, there is often a disconnect—a sense of dissatisfaction and friction. If you have a solid sense of what you value—what you believe you stand for—then you can choose opportunities that feel right to you.

It's also important to remember that although our core values may remain pretty much the same across our lives and career, there may be some changes and shifts, given our current life situation. For example, at the age of twenty-one, some people may value adventure, novelty, freedom, and frequent changes in location or job choices. However, at the age of thirty-five, some of these same people may find that they value stability, family, and more of a sense of routine in their lives. The reverse can also be true. Life, lifestyle, health, and shifting career circumstances can impact our values. So when thinking about your own values, it is important to consider what is important to you *now*—as opposed to what was important to you when you first began pursuing your profession. You may find your values haven't shifted much—or, you may find that you have a much different perspective today than you did at another point in your life. Pay attention to what matters to you *now* in determining which opportunities to pursue.

 **Notes to Myself**

**Check out the list below and circle your top seven values.** This list is a compilation of values listed on MindTools.com[23] and JamesClear.com,[24] and from my own coaching work. You can also visit the US Department of Labor for additional examples of values.[25]

As you look through the list, feel free to add other values that are important to you that may not be included here. If you wish to add additional values, pencil them in on the four blank lines you will see at the end of the list of values I've included here. If you're wondering what a precise definition of any of these values might be, use your own definition/interpretation of the value to guide you.

 **Notes to Myself**

**First, circle your top seven values. Once you've circled your top seven values, go back and prioritize the values you've just circled. Which is your #1 value, your #2 value—all the way down through your #7 value. Number the ones you've circled accordingly.**

| | | | |
|---|---|---|---|
| Accountability | Community | Effectiveness | Happiness |
| Accuracy | Compassion | Efficiency | Hard Work |
| Achievement | Competition | Empathy | Health |
| Adventure | Consistency | Enthusiasm | Helping Society |
| Altruism | Contribution | Equality | Honesty |
| Ambition | Control | Excellence | Independence |
| Assertiveness | Cooperation | Expertise | Intellectual Status |
| Balance | Creativity | Exploration | Intelligence |
| Belonging | Curiosity | Expressiveness | Intuition |
| Boldness | Decisiveness | Fairness | Joy |
| Calmness | Dependability | Fun | Justice |
| Challenge | Determination | Generosity | Leadership |
| Collegiality | Diligence | Grace | Learning |
| Commitment | Diversity | Growth | Loyalty |

| | | | |
|---|---|---|---|
| Making a Difference | Professionalism | Spontaneity | Tolerance |
| Mastery | Relationships | Stability | Trustworthiness |
| Meaningful Work | Resourcefulness | Strength | Understanding |
| Openness | Security | Success | Uniqueness |
| Optimism | Self-reliance | Support | Usefulness |
| Order | Service | Teamwork | Vision |
| Practicality | Simplicity | Timeliness | Vitality |

_____ _____ _____ _____

**Next, list those seven prioritized values in the spaces below.**

_____ _____ _____ _____

_____ _____ _____

How did you do? Any surprises? As you look at your prioritized list, reflect on how well you are able to live and work in line with the values you hold most dear. Completing a "values" exercise often brings us more clarity about how we might like to do things differently in our daily lives to better reflect our values. Completing an exercise like this one also reaffirms what is most important to us.

• • •

### View of the Future

We all hold some vision of the future—but we differ as individuals in *how* we see the future—especially our own personal future. For some people, the future is far away, out of sight, and not thought about very much; for them, the present matters most. And for others, the past occupies most of their thoughts, especially if the past was a happier time than the present. In some instances, one's view of the future can be influenced by age. If you're seventy, you may see only the past and assume that a major part of your life is already over. The future may seem shortened without much in the way of "new beginnings."

But any view of the future is quite personal and dependent, in some respects, on one's attitude—a topic we covered earlier. I've talked with professionals who believe that most of the "good stuff" in life has already happened by the time they turn thirty—with little to look forward to after that. And I've talked with people in their early eighties who are bursting with life and can't wait to see what tomorrow brings.

Why is your vision of the future important in choosing growth opportunities? First: If you have an optimistic, positive vision of the future and your place in it, you're much more likely to be interested in finding ways to grow and excel. Second: You'll probably plan more and be more discerning in deciding how you want to spend your time. Third: The more detailed your picture of the future is, the more you'll want to do your best to shape it—and that goes for your own career, your profession, and the causes you believe in.

Here is what I have found to be true in working with scores of professionals over the years when it comes to discussions about their view of the future. Regardless of age, or current level of employment, those who tend to see their future as big, in terms of potential—maybe even bigger than their present—tend to be excited about what's around the corner. Sure, they are a bit anxious too, but mostly they look forward to shaping that future and to anticipating it in any way they can.

Think about it—if you can look forward positively, think like a futurist (more on this in chapter 5) and see yourself as someone with value to offer to your profession, it's likely that more opportunities will open up to you. Of course, you won't want to keep these things to yourself. You'll want to make certain others know that the future is a place in which you see yourself excelling.

### Aspirations

This area can be a tricky one to assess. So consider these points before filling in your response to the questions in this section. We all have (or had, at one time) aspirations for where we'd like to take our careers and our professional lives. But as John Lennon (and Allen Saunders before him) put it, "Life happens when you're making other plans."[26] Think back to your days immediately following your graduation. You may have had a clear picture in mind of exactly what you'd like to be doing in your new field. Or you may have graduated without any certainty at that point about how or where exactly you'd like to pursue your profession. Then over time and through trial and error, multiple positions, or serendipity, you landed in your sweet spot—and you found yourself thrilled to be doing what felt "just right." Or you may find that what once thrilled and excited you at twenty-two no longer holds your passion at the age of thirty-five. Or you may still be hoping to find that place in your field that feels like home—because your "dream" position hasn't shown up yet, or you were downsized out of it due to budget cutbacks.

While we all likely formed some sort of career aspirations early in our career— very clear ones or fuzzy ideas about how we'd like to be a part of our field—so much can happen on our way to our dreams. Unfulfilled aspirations can cause us to grow disillusioned, give up hope, or find that the dream we once pursued no longer fits who we are today. Even fulfilled aspirations may have us asking if there's anything more out there. That's only natural as we evolve over time as individuals and as professionals.

No matter what your circumstances, aspirations remain important; they offer meaning, passion, and engagement. If you're living out your aspirations at the current moment, outstanding! If your early aspirations have fallen by the wayside or if they got lost a while back, it doesn't mean they should dry up or disappear. Quite the opposite—taking the time to consider what your aspirations are *now* is very worthwhile. To aspire is a powerful act. So think about your own current aspirations, but leave out specific job locations or specific job titles. Simply consider how you'd like to move toward your best and brightest self.

## Notes to Myself

**Describe your professional aspirations at the present time.** You may have a fuzzy vision of what you'd like to be doing, or you may be able to very clearly articulate it. Either way, take the time to really reflect on this question before you respond.

_____

_____

_____

_____

### Time/Energy/Commitments

In a perfect world, we would have the time and energy to accomplish everything we set out to do—with plenty of time and energy left over to spend with the people and causes that matter most to us. But that's not going to happen. You've probably noticed that the word *balance* isn't tossed about quite so frequently these days, since balance often seems like a luxury—or perhaps, mission impossible. Even the notion of multitasking has been debunked by the research, at least when it comes to engaging in multiple higher-order cognitive tasks.

How do you add another activity—pursuing growth opportunities—to your already overflowing inbox? The answer: you do so judiciously and strategically. If you aren't thoughtful about adding additional items to your to-do list, other things drop off, or you find that you're doing your latest added-on tasks with some level of resentment or you hurry through them. Not helpful at all! The whole point of this book is to present ways that you can pursue and leverage the right growth opportunities by either melding them into the life you are living right now or adding them to your current professional development in a way that helps you grow and gives you joy.

*Passion and Meaning*

These two words aren't generally included in a self-assessment. They can't be measured or assessed in the way we measure or assess other things like knowledge or skills. That is as it should be. Passion and meaning give color, juice, and intention to our lives. And they are different for each of us. So when considering where we want to put our effort and our time, based on what we feel is most important to us, it makes good sense to first understand where our passion lies and what gives meaning to our work.

Before you go any further, think about what you feel passionate about—it may be your family, your community, or a cause that you strongly believe in. Next, consider when, where, and under what circumstances you feel most passionate about your work. I've talked with many library staff members over the years who have expressed a wide range of things they are passionate about: advocacy, accessibility, outreach, the community they serve, and the ability to help those on their journey to literacy.

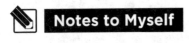 **Notes to Myself**

**List three things (ideas, ideals, causes, issues, and so on) that you are most passionate about. Be sure that one of these is related to your field.**

_____

_____

_____

**Now list three things that you believe add meaning to your life. Again, be sure that one of these is related to what makes your work (or some aspect of your field) meaningful to you.**

_____

_____

_____

Now that you have written these two important areas down, consider them a compass for you as you choose opportunities.

### Risk-Taking Orientation

What's the first thing you think of when you read the words *risk-taking*? Reckless? Scary? Intriguing? Curious to hear more? Risk-taking can conjure up any of these thoughts—it just depends on the risk . . . and on your feelings about the whole idea of taking a risk. Some like to play it safe, keep their heads down, and avoid doing anything that might jeopardize their status quo. They might describe themselves as risk-averse. Others might jump at the chance to take a risk, as they see the risk as an exciting chance to experiment. The best risk-takers, at least when it comes to professional moves, are the ones who are willing to consider risks as part of their strategy to move their careers ahead, provided they have weighed the risks and determined what they are risking and how much value the risk holds for them. They are prudent risk-takers—not haphazard, all-or-nothing kinds of risk-takers.

This last group (the prudent risk-takers) tends to think of risks in the way that Sandra Peterson, group worldwide chair at Johnson & Johnson, does. Writer Julie Zeilinger describes Peterson in this way: she reframes risk as "an opportunity to succeed rather than a path to failure."[27] The smartest risk-takers understand that action, rather than a passive stance on their part, is most often required to take full advantage of an opportunity. But it's not an impulsive, spur-of-the-moment type of risk-taking.

To make risk-taking a smart move for you, you need to see it as part of a larger picture—one in which you've thought strategically about how you want to grow and know which opportunities are worth the investment of time, energy, and risk on your part.

**Notes to Myself**

**What is your overall feeling about taking risks?**

_____

_____

_____

**When was the last time you took a risk in your career? Describe what you did.**

_____

_____

_____

**What was the outcome?**

_____

_____

_____

**If you haven't taken any risks so far in moving your career forward, why might that be the case?**

_____

_____

_____

**What kinds of risks might you consider worth taking at this point in your career? Which risks would not be worth taking? (It's important to be able to distinguish between the two.)**

_____

_____

_____

Remember—a risk need not involve putting your whole career on the line, moving to the other side of the world, or taking on an assignment that you're clearly not ready for or interested in. Go forward with your risk-taking in a way that works for you—just go!

We've covered a lot of territory in this chapter. And you've done a great deal of thinking and reflecting to get you this far. But you'll see in the chapters coming up just how important this up-front work is to get you ready for leveraging the right opportunities.

## Notes

1. Erin Palmer, "Guest Post: The Importance of Self-Assessments," Benoit Central, May 17, 2012, http://benoitconsulting.com/guest-post-the-importance-of-self-assessments/.
2. Peter Drucker, "Managing Oneself," *Harvard Business Review*, January 2005, 202–12.
3. F. John Reh, "Understanding Knowledge, Skills and Abilities: KSA," *The Balance*, September 10, 2017, www.thebalance.com/understanding-knowledge-skills-and-abilities-ksa-2275329/.
4. Ibid.
5. San Jose State University, "School of Information," Core Courses and Electives, http://ischool.sjsu.edu/current-students/courses/core-courses-and-electives/.
6. Reh, "Understanding Knowledge."
7. Ibid.
8. Ian Leslie, *Curious: The Desire to Know and Why Your Future Depends on It* (Philadelphia: Basic Books, 2015).
9. Ibid.
10. Ibid., 152–53.
11. Seth Godin, *Linchpin: Are You Indispensable?* (New York: Penguin Group, 2010), 55.
12. Oxford Dictionaries, "Savvy," https://en.oxforddictionaries.com/definition/savvy/.
13. Reh, "Understanding Knowledge."
14. Alison Doyle, "What Are Soft Skills?," *The Balance*, April 14, 2018, www.thebalance.com/what-are-soft-skills-2060852.
15. Jennifer Jarratt, personal communication with the author, 2000.
16. Alison Doyle, "What Are the Hard Skills Employers Seek?," *The Balance*, April 17, 2018, www.thebalance.com/what-are-hard-skills-2060829/.
17. American Library Association, ALA Job List, https://joblist.ala.org/.
18. MyWorldofWork.com, "What Are My Strengths?," www.myworldofwork.co.uk/my-career-options/what-are-my-strengths/.
19. Tom Rath, *StrengthsFinder 2.0* (Omaha, NE: Gallup Press, 2007).
20. Dictionary.com, "Attitude," www.dictionary.com/browse/attitude?s=t/.
21. Heath Row, "Coping-Martin Seligman," *Fast Company Magazine*, November 30, 1998, www.fastcompany.com/35969/coping-martin-seligman/.
22. Jon Acuff, *Do Over: Make Today the First Day of Your New Career* (New York: Penguin, 2017), 108.
23. MindTools.com, "What Are Your Values?," www.mindtools.com/pages/article/newTED_85.htm.
24. James Clear, "Core-Value List," https://jamesclear.com/core-values/.
25. US Department of Labor, "What Are Values?," www.careeronestop.org/ExploreCareers/Assessments/work-values.aspx.
26. Wikipedia.org, "Allen Saunders," https://en.wikipedia.org/wiki/Allen_Saunders/.
27. Julie Zeilinger, "7 Reasons Why Risk-Taking Leads to Success," in *Huffington Post*, September 25, 2017, www.huffingtonpost.com/2013/08/13/seven-reasons-why-risk-taking-leads-to-success_n_3749425.html.

## CHAPTER 5

· · · · · · · · ·

# How Well Do You Know What's New and What's Next?

uthor Seth Godin is 100 percent right when he lays out this challenge: "The best future available to us is a future where you contribute your true self and your best work. Are you up for that?"[1] The ability to contribute your best work and your best self goes a long way to creating a future where you are employable, valued, and passionate about what you are doing. However, I would add that it's also critical to know and understand the shape of that future you're heading toward. Not by gazing into a crystal ball, reading some tea leaves, or simply trying to guess, but by taking the time to engage in two very important activities: first, make it a practice to take a wide-angle perspective as you approach your work, your field, the world around you, and possible opportunities going forward; and second, learn the work- and career-related trends that futurists and workplace forecasters are highlighting right now. Then as you become accustomed to taking this larger perspective and learning about key trends, the smartest thing you can do is reflect on what this treasure trove of information and insight holds for you professionally.

Before going any further, let me make a small correction. So far, I've been emphasizing the importance of considering your "future"—when actually, I should be using the word "futures." That's because we all have many possible futures ahead of us. I'm not talking about an episode of *Twilight Zone* here; nor am I suggesting you consider parallel universes where you could experience multiple futures. The truth is that each one of us can look forward to multiple possibilities in the future depending on what we do or don't do—and what the world around us does or doesn't do as it faces challenges and opportunities socially, technologically, economically, environmentally, and politically. Depending on our actions and that of the world around us, many different scenarios could play out. That's why I use the word *futures* to suggest many different options. When futurists talk about futures, they often refer to possible, probable, and preferred futures. Alida Draudt and Julia Rose West refer to this as the "cone of possibilities" in which the *possible* futures include all possible futures that are open for consideration. *Probable* futures include ones that are most likely to happen, given your current trajectory (those things likely to happen in your life if you keep going in the direction you are now, without any huge changes in the world around you impacting you). *Preferable* futures, according to Draudt and West, are "also within the realm of the possible, but not necessarily within the realm of the probable. This is your intentional and desirable future."[2] In other words, it is your intentional action—along with adapting to changes around you that may impact you—that leads to a preferred future. So consider many possibilities as you move forward—and many ways that you can shape your future, starting right now. Why is this so important? Consider this: since we don't know (with any certainty) how the future will unfold, it is a very good idea to be prepared for different futures that may occur. We can do this by thoughtfully considering a range of possibilities, and then we can take actions in the present that can move us toward a future that we prefer.

Up to this point, you've taken a good amount of time to more fully understand yourself in terms of your strengths, skills, and other attributes that you bring to the table. You also have had the opportunity to gain a solid understanding of what "the work that needs doing" means, along with information about the current state of the workplace and your field. The two key puzzle pieces that we'll focus on in this chapter—learning to think like a futurist and understanding and leveraging key trends—will pull everything together. These key pieces are especially helpful before you choose and begin to implement the growth opportunities you want to pursue.

## Think Like a Futurist

It's likely you have heard the term *futurist* before. You may even have some acquaintances who are futurists. To make sure we all have the same understanding of who futurists are and what they do, let's briefly go into some detail about the work they focus on. Professional futurists are not fortune tellers, wild speculators, or those who engage in wild visions about *the* future that's going to impact us all in the days, weeks, and months to come.

Professional futurists' focus is within the academic field of futures studies. They learn the theories and recognized tools of futurists and forecasters, which include the study and analysis of trends, scenario planning, forecasting, and backcasting, among others. They often consult with organizations to help them anticipate the future and be ready to adapt to it and engage with it rather than simply react to it.

In the same way that professional futurists do their work on behalf of their organizational clients, you can think like a futurist on behalf of yourself and your own career. It's a matter of learning about some of the tools that professional futurists use and adapting them to your own situation. It's also about committing to some attitudes and behaviors that allow space for more opportunities to emerge. There are several ways you can do this. The next section of this chapter focuses on five in greater detail.

## Be Curious

Remember when we were kids and spent a good part of each day asking questions? We wanted to know *why?* Or *why not?* Or *how?* Or *what if?* The questions never stopped, and usually we delighted in the process of trying to figure things out. There is magic in being curious. Yet as adults, we sometimes forget the excitement in *not* knowing that we once reveled in. And of course, there is also the issue of being expected to know the answers to most questions that comes with being an adult. This expectation is even higher for those in LIS, where everyone else is asking questions of you!

Curiosity is a skill that we need to get back in touch with as we move toward the future. Doesn't it seem like you're seeing new phrases or terms or hearing about yet one more new technology almost every day? I know that's true for myself and most of my colleagues. I bet it's true for you too. Our curiosity can keep us motivated to figure out what these new terms and technologies are all about.

When we're curious, we allow ourselves to imagine things differently. Of course, it's natural to drift toward what is familiar, known, and comfortable; but when we're curious, we give ourselves permission to look beyond what we currently know—we let ourselves play with possibilities. And that includes being curious enough to try new approaches to problems or challenges that we may have faced before.

For example, here is how Laverne, a woman I was doing some career coaching with, put her curiosity to work for her. Laverne was in job-search mode. She knew she was ready to move on from her current role at the library she worked in. At first, she relied on the same approach she had always used in the past—she scanned job openings online and in her association newsletters, focusing on the same type of job titles she had used when searching in the past. The more Laverne and I talked, the clearer it became to both of us that Laverne wanted to expand the type of work she did and also make use of some skill sets that she didn't get to use in her current role. So we brainstormed a new strategy: Laverne decided that she would expand her search to include new and different job titles and focus on postings that included some different skill sets beyond what she had been doing most recently (these other skill sets were ones she was quite competent in—she just had never thought in this more expanded way before). Guess what happened? She landed a position as a business intelligence researcher. No mention of "librarian" in the job announcement or job title—yet the position let her use a skill set she already had in a new environment that excited her. I'm not suggesting that you need to move to a new setting to find satisfaction in your job and use the skills you want to use. What I *am* suggesting is that being curious about opportunities, asking questions, and remaining committed to looking at things through "new eyes" can pay off.

Here is one more benefit of being curious—and this one involves being curious about the knowledge and expertise of others. One thing that I bet we can all agree on as we move forward is that it's pretty clear that the world will continue to move faster, become more complex, and change even more rapidly than it has up until now. In such a world—and workplace—we cannot know everything. It's just not possible. But while we can accept and appreciate what we *do* know, we can also become more curious about what others, like our colleagues and those with expertise in other areas, bring to the table. The work of the future will likely be done best when we collaborate with others and pool our knowledge. But first we have to become curious about what others can contribute and what we can create together.

## Don't Always Rely on the Past to Guide Your Future

I bet I can guess what you're thinking right now, and it may go something like this: I've learned a lot from my past experiences—why wouldn't I use that information to guide me in creating my future? And you're right . . . to a certain degree.

Let me explain a dilemma we all face when trying to imagine possibilities in the future. In a fascinating study done at Washington University, psychologists Karl Szpunar and Kathleen McDermott were trying to determine how people like you and me imagined the past and the future.[3] So they connected their study participants up to fMRI machines and asked them two questions. First, they asked their subjects to imagine an event from their past. While the study participants were doing this, the researchers took pictures of their brains to see what areas of the brain lit up during this activity. Then they asked the same study participants to imagine a future event—and again they took pictures of the subjects' brains to see what areas were activated during *this* activity. Can you guess what the researchers discovered? They found that the same neural network lit up—whether people were recalling a past event or envisioning a future event. What does this mean? From this experiment, the researchers were able to conclude that we rely on our memories to form vivid images of the future.

At this point, you may be saying to yourself: *So what?* Well, actually, the *so what* is very interesting! According to Szpunar and McDermott, we tend to see the future as a progression of the past.[4] This, in turn, makes it more challenging to imagine a future that's a whole lot different than our past. Other futurists have pointed out a similar dilemma that they refer to as our "permanent present." They note that if we assume that tomorrow, next week, and next year will roll out just like it rolled out today—in other words, without much happening that's different—then it's also difficult to imagine a different future. Can you see how this can stifle our thinking about new possibilities?

So what are we to do if we want to imagine other, different, novel, and innovative options for ourselves? Many futurists suggest that we can intentionally push past these assumptions that we carry with us. We can broaden our thinking to encompass new ideas and new areas of interest. By engaging in meaningful conversations with those who may be outside our customary group of colleagues, we can gain a wider appreciation of those who have other areas of expertise. By reading different books and different blogs, by traveling to new places and choosing new areas to explore, we shift things. And interesting things begin to happen—we start making new connections between things that may not appear to have anything to do with one another, and we start imagining new possibilities. These are our "AHA!" moments—our insights that lead us down new paths.

## Make Creativity, Imagination, and Play a Part of Your Mindset

This may be another one of those times when you're thinking something like, *That sounds great, but with all the things on my desk at the moment, play and imagination aren't at the top of my to-do list*. And I do understand why you might be thinking that. But stay with me for a few minutes more on this one.

If you're committed to thinking like a futurist on behalf of your career, then the notion of play, creativity, and imagination are essential. Unless, of course, you want to keep the same-old, same-old thing going. Those who are successful—and by that, I mean doing work they truly enjoy and that makes a difference—are ones who approach their work with a playfulness and imagination that engage and energize them.

In the same way, creativity can engage us and push us into trying new approaches or techniques—even to the things we do day after day. Perhaps it means responding to a coworker or a student or even a challenging client in a new way. Maybe it means turning an established routine on its head. Possibly, it means starting from scratch to design an outreach program that's unlike anything that's been done before. Or it could simply mean proposing to your supervisor a new approach you'd like to try out on a small scale in your current work setting. It means, ultimately, giving yourself permission to experiment and shift "the way you've always done something." Go for it—and see what happens. And if you truly believe that your work environment leaves little room to be creative and imaginative, don't forget that there are plenty of opportunities outside your workplace to put your creativity to work—including associations, speaking groups, community groups, and more.

## Backcast Your Way to Your Future

*Backcasting* starts with a specific future outcome and then works backward to the present conditions, according to BusinessDictionary.com.[5]

It's quite likely you're familiar with the term *forecasting*—the act of looking forward and predicting what's coming at some point in the future—whether it's the weather, the most popular video game this coming season, or the likelihood that a particular sports team will do well. The focus is on "seeing" into the future.

But backcasting takes the opposite perspective. To backcast is to first specify a certain point in time in the future (e.g., three years from now) and then describe a certain preferred thing happening in that time period (e.g., graduation from an MLIS program or completion of a postmaster's certificate program from a school of information). Then working backward from that point, the idea is to determine what one needs to do to reach that preferred future. If you've ever "worked backward" on a problem or an idea that you'd like to see become a reality, you've probably done some backcasting.

Futurists use this tool to help clients get more concrete about actions they'll need to take to get to a preferred future they are envisioning for their organization. One advantage of backcasting is that when we do it, because we're working backward rather than starting out with the present moment, we're less constrained by current challenges and realities. We're less likely to say "yes, but I can't do that—I'm too busy," or "I can't possibly do that, I don't have the resources."

Here is a good example of how backcasting could work for you in growing your career.

Let's say that a preferred future you envision for yourself in three years is taking on more leadership responsibilities within the public library sector. In other words, you want to be in a leadership role in three years. So using a backcasting-focused approach, this is how you might proceed to that preferred future you want for yourself. Look at figure 5.1, and follow it from *right to left*.

This example is, obviously, an abbreviated version of what your own backcasting diagram would look like. The person in the example would, quite likely, have other

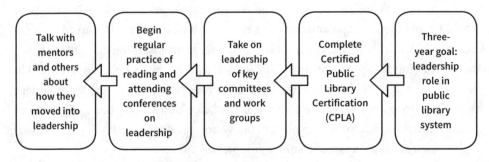

**Figure 5.1.** Backcasting example

steps that would be included, such as participating in leadership-related podcasts, taking on some leadership roles in her community, or identifying a sponsor who could guide her through the intricacies of moving into leadership within a public library system. Or the person might request more opportunities to supervise or direct the work of others within his current position. Everyone who tries backcasting will have a different series of steps leading from what they want to be doing and what actions they will take to get there. Notice that you create your "backcast" diagram *from right to left*, but once you've completed your backcasting "diagram" by filling in all the steps needed to reach your goal, you will take the necessary actions moving from *left to right*—starting with step 1 (whatever you need to do now) to begin your journey to your ultimate goal.

## Play with Scenarios

We've all played with scenarios before—we just didn't label them that way. Every time we reflect on "what if" possibilities, we are, in a way, playing out scenarios in our minds. *"What if" the car breaks down? "What if" I can't get a sitter for Saturday night? "What if" I get to go on that vacation I've been planning for so long and it rains every day?* The list goes on and on. In each instance, we're considering what we would or would not do, what the implications might be, and how our lives might be affected. But sometimes our "what if" thinking keeps us stuck as we obsess over "what if" worries that we can't seem to resolve, or we fantasize about a "what if" wished-for future, but don't take our daydreams about it any further than getting lost in our thoughts. It's possible to do more with the "what if" moments you have—especially as they relate to growing your career. How? By putting your "what ifs" to work for you through adapting a tool that futurists frequently use—scenarios.

Scenarios, according to Richard Lum, professional futurist and author, "are descriptions of alternative possible futures." Lum emphasizes that generating scenarios is not about predicting the future or trying to identify *the one* future that will come to pass. Rather, generating scenarios is a way to play with possibilities, given different possible futures.[6]

Here is a quick playful exercise that will give you a closer look at scenarios (though in a very abbreviated fashion).

- Imagine a time in the future: let's say fifteen years from now.
- Next, imagine four ways that future (fifteen years from now) might look different.

For instance, fifteen years from now, our world may be pretty much as it is now—without many changes. Or, it could be much different—better in ways we couldn't have expected. Or, it could be different than the present because it's worse than we could have expected. Or, finally, the world around us in fifteen years could be so different we couldn't even imagine or grasp the magnitude of the changes that have occurred—it would be as though everything we knew got turned upside down! (One futurist, Jamais Cascio, refers to this as being a "weirder than I expected" future).[7] These examples, taken together, could be considered four different scenarios for our future.

Now imagine what types of opportunities each of these scenarios might offer us. For example, imagine that scenario fifteen years from now in which our world is much better than we expected. Perhaps it's one in which librarianship and information services skills are in demand across all sectors of the economy—one in which organizations of all types are trying to recruit LIS professionals for all sorts of new jobs. (*Nice picture, isn't it?*) Under those circumstances, what types of opportunities might be open to you? Where might you want to use your talents? How would you like to make a difference? Scenario planning exercises give you the chance to imagine different possible futures and then imagine how you might prepare for and thrive in those futures. Scenario planning lets you stretch your "what if" thinking—to get you to consider what opportunities might be out there that you could pursue, given all sorts of alternative possibilities. If you're interested in learning more about scenarios, check out some of the great ideas for scenario planning from Cascio that you'll find online.[8]

## Become Trend-Savvy

Another way to understand what's new and what's next and to take advantage of that knowledge is to know and leverage the trends that are just around the corner (as well as those just starting to appear on the horizon). If you take the time to reflect on the trends that have been identified as being important to your field, as well as the ones that have been identified outside your field, you gain valuable insight into key growth opportunities for yourself. It's imperative to become trend-savvy so you can adapt, anticipate, and grow your career accordingly.

## Trends in Libraries and Librarianship

Remember in chapter 1 when we looked back (way back!) at the work that needed doing during different time periods in the past? Now we're going to look in the other direction—the future. In the next section, you'll learn about the latest trends in libraries and librarianship that have been compiled by the ALA's Center for the Future of Libraries, which is directed by Miguel Figueroa. Here is how the center describes its work:

> The Center for the Future of Libraries works to identify trends relevant to libraries and librarianship. This collection is available to help libraries and librarians understand how trends are developing and why they matter. Each trend is updated as new reports and articles are made available. New trends will be added as they are developed.[9]

There are thirty current trends listed on the Center for the Future of Libraries webpage (www.ala.org/tools/future/trends). After each trend, you will see a brief definition of it, taken directly from the Center for the Future of Libraries web pages, along with some space to answer the questions posed in the next section as they relate to that trend. Read each trend, take the time to reflect on it, look at the questions below, and write in your response before going on to the next trend. Reflecting and writing down your responses are the surest ways to maximize your learning here. Also be sure to look at a fuller explanation of each trend, information on how each trend is developing, why it matters to libraries and librarianship as well as to information services and organizations, and additional notes and resources at www.ala.org/tools/future/trends.

You may find that you'll have a lengthier response for some trends than you do for others. That may be because you are more drawn to certain trends as you find them more interesting, more appealing, or more in line with opportunities that you can see for yourself. That's fine—just try to fill in some notation for each one and then go into depth on the particular ones that seem most relevant to your career going forward.

 **Notes to Myself**

As you read through the list of trends that follows, ask yourself

- So what?
- What does this trend mean to me in terms of my everyday work?
- What relevance does this trend have for my career going forward?
- What potential growth opportunities might be contained within this trend?
- What work will need doing now and in the near future as this trend becomes more of an everyday reality?

**Aging Advances**: An aging workforce and population will change the United States and other developed nations, impacting the workplace, government budgets, policy, family life, and more.

_____

_____

_____

**Anonymity**: Long a hallmark of communication on the Internet, anonymity is a promoted feature of applications (Whisper, Secret) and forums (Reddit) allowing users to share information secretly. Understanding the role anonymity plays in free speech and intellectual freedom may become increasingly important for libraries and librarians.

_____

_____

_____

**Badging**: Badging, and digital badges in particular, offer opportunities to recognize individuals' accomplishments, skills, qualities, or interests and help set goals, motivate behavior, represent achievements, and communicate success in learning offered in schools, professional settings, or daily life.[10]

_____

_____

_____

**Basic Income**: Basic income—frequently referred to as universal basic income—is a payment from the government to all people in society, regardless of their income or work circumstances, meant to guarantee basic needs like food and shelter as well as enable individuals to pursue their self-improvement and contributions to society.

_____

_____

_____

**Blockchain**: Blockchain technology uses a distributed database (multiple devices not connected to a common processor) that organizes data into records (blocks) that have cryptographic validation and are timestamped and linked to previous records so that they can only be changed by those who own the encryption keys to write to the files.

_____

_____

_____

**Collective Impact**: In the face of limited resources and persistent, big social issues (hunger, poverty, violence, education, health, public safety, the environment), organizations from different sectors are adopting common agendas to combat issues within their communities.

_____

_____

_____

**Connected Learning**: Social and digital media available via the Internet connects students and young people to each other and to a host of formal and informal educators, providing limitless opportunities to seek and acquire new knowledge and skills. Connected learning is learning that is "highly social, interest-driven, and oriented toward educational, economic, or civic opportunity."[11]

_____

_____

_____

**Connected Toys**: A new crop of toys take advantage of trends in wireless connectivity, the Internet of things, artificial intelligence, and machine learning to create highly personalized exchanges between object and child.

_____

_____

_____

**Creative Placemaking**: Creative placemaking brings together partners from public, private, nonprofit, and community sectors to strategically shape the physical and social character of a public space through arts and cultural activities that encourage public discourse, neighborhood development, community health and safety, social justice, economic growth, environmental sustainability, civic pride, and an authentic "sense of place."[12]

_____

_____

_____

**Data Everywhere**: Data collection and management is not a new trend, but new technologies have greatly improved the opportunities to collect, store, and analyze customer data and personal information. The explosion of mobile devices, Internet-connected devices, and applications has drastically increased opportunities for data collection. As data is collected, companies and organizations can use the information to develop products and services, improve marketing and communications, or monetize information.

_____

_____

_____

**Digital Natives**: Children and young people born into and raised in a digital world (post 1980) may work, study, and interact in very different ways from "digital immigrants," those who were born just a generation before.

_____

_____

_____

**Drones**: Drones or "unmanned aerial vehicles" (UAVs) will become a regular part of life, used in research, transportation and delivery, artistic production, news coverage and reporting, law enforcement and surveillance, and entertainment.

_____

_____

_____

**Emerging Adulthood**: Emerging adulthood considers the period from the late teens through twenties as a time of distinct psychological and behavioral characteristics that in more affluent countries may result in individuals' taking longer to move out of their parents' home, involve themselves in a career, get married, and have children.

_____

_____

_____

**Fandom**: Fandom refers to a community of people who are passionate about something, whether it's a film, a band, a television show, a book, or a sports team.[13] The growing availability of media and social networks has provided individuals more opportunities to discover content and then more easily find groups of like-minded people with whom they can share and exchange proof of their fandom (discussions, writing, art, etc.).

_____

_____

_____

**Fast Casual**: Fast casual is a new and growing concept in restaurants, positioned between quick-service restaurants (QSRs), like McDonald's, Burger King, or KFC, and casual restaurants, such as Denny's, Applebee's, or Chili's. The fast-casual concept's hallmarks include counter service, customized menus, freshly prepared and higher-quality foods, and upscale and inviting dining spaces.

_____

_____

_____

**Flipped Learning**: Flipped learning—or flipped classrooms, backward classrooms, inverted classrooms, or reverse teaching—utilizes a model where students review content online via video lectures and assignments are completed during class meeting times with students and teachers working through and solving questions together.

---

**Gamification**: Gamification (the application of game elements and digital game design techniques to non-game settings) and game-based learning (game playing that has defined learning outcomes) are seeing greater adoption and recognition in educational and professional settings.

---

**Haptic Technology**: Haptic technology, haptic feedback, or simply haptics, is technology that incorporates tactile experience or feedback as part of its user interface, creating a sense of touch through vibrations, motion, or other forces.

---

*Income Inequality*: President Barack Obama has called income inequality the "defining challenge of our time."[14] According to the Institute for Policy Studies, income inequality refers to the extent to which income is distributed in an uneven manner among a population—and in the United States, income inequality has been growing markedly for the past 30 years.[15]

_____

_____

_____

*Internet of Things*: Smaller computing and radio devices, often unseen or built into objects, will sense and transmit data offering greater control of and connectivity between objects.

_____

_____

_____

*Maker Movement*: Do-it-yourselfers, tinkerers, hackers, entrepreneurs, and interested learners are finding opportunities to make what they want and determine their own creative paths. Makers take advantage of the availability of new technology and traditional craft tools, improved communication between community members, and new pathways to the marketplace (sharing economies, e-commerce, crowdsourcing).

_____

_____

_____

**Privacy Shifting**: The way that society and individuals value privacy will change, especially as technologies require the supply of more and more personal information; become smaller, cheaper, and more available; or monitor users and connect to the Internet. Individuals will need to balance their value for privacy with the benefits of these new technologies.

_____

_____

_____

**Resilience**: "Resilience" or "resiliency" incorporates preparations for and rapid recovery from physical, social, and economic disruptions, including environmental disasters, terrorist attacks, or economic collapse.[16]

_____

_____

_____

**Robots**: Robots will move from industrial and factory settings, where they were first introduced in the early 1960s, to more everyday work, educational, research, and living spaces. These collaborative robots will increasingly perform repetitive tasks and work alongside humans.

_____

_____

_____

**Sharing Economy**: Traditional models of ownership are changing. A sharing economy (also referred to as collaborative consumption or peer-to-peer collaboration or rental), often utilizing social technologies, allows users to share resources, goods, services, and even skills.

_____

_____

_____

**Short Reading**: Formats that take advantage of short opportunities to read help encourage reading among those who are pressed for time, reluctant to read, or distracted by technology.

_____

_____

_____

**Unplugged**: In a world where information and technology are everywhere and ever-present, opportunities to unplug may become more essential, benefiting both professional and personal experiences.

_____

_____

_____

**Urbanization**: More and more people will migrate to urban areas, resulting in both the growth of existing urban areas and the urbanization of suburban areas or the greater integration of suburban areas into larger metro areas.

_____

_____

_____

***Virtual Reality***: Virtual reality—the computer-generated simulation of images or whole environments that can be experienced using special electronic equipment—is progressing in several ways, including traditional virtual reality that creates environments that allow people to be "present" in an alternative environment; augmented reality that starts with the real world and overlays virtual objects and information; and spherical or 360-degree video that captures an entire scene in which the viewer can look up, down, and around.[17]

---

---

---

***Voice Control***: Advances in machine learning, speech recognition, and natural language understanding will drive the development of virtual assistants and bots that act more and more like people, controlled by and responding with human voices and fulfilling search queries, acting as proxies, accomplishing tasks, and asking questions of us in return.[18]

---

---

---

You should now have a greater understanding of "what's around the corner" when it comes to trends in your field. That knowledge puts you out in front of many who stay too focused on the present and hope the future will take care of itself. Keeping an eye on workplace and career-related trends is another excellent way to enhance your career smarts.

*(Material from this section of chapter 5, "Trends in Libraries and Librarianship," is reprinted with permission from the ALA, Center for the Future of Libraries, www.ala.org/tools/future/trends).*

# Trends in Career and the Workplace

Now that you've had the opportunity to review and reflect on trends inside your field, it's time to look outside. By paying attention to what's new and next in areas beyond your own, you can add to your professional savvy even more. Look at the highlights of workplace- and career-related trends for 2018 (and likely beyond) from author Dan Schwabel. For more details and a full list of his selected trends, I encourage you to read the entire article that has been posted online by *Forbes*.[19]

To maximize your learning from a review of these trends, I suggest you reflect on each trend in the same way you did for "Trends in Libraries and Librarianship," in the earlier section.

1. *Lifelong learning* (in some form) will continue to be essential with an increased number of entities (beyond traditional educational institutions) offering courses, credentials, and certifications. Along with traditional degrees, more workers (particularly younger ones) are considering shorter-term courses to pick up new skills.

2. *Organizations will focus on helping their current employees to "upskill"* (bring their skills up-to-date to meet current needs). Part of this effort is to retain workers; it also represents a way for employers to reduce the skills gap.

3. *AI (artificial intelligence) will become more prevalent in the workplace*, including the use of chatbots to provide help in a variety of ways: answering employee questions, looking up product info, and helping with on-demand customer service.

4. *Financial and mental wellness* will become more "top-of-mind" issues for organizations. With so many employees struggling with financial issues (like paying back student loans), as well as workers dealing with mental health issues (like burnout or depression), more companies are offering employees ways to help them get through these challenges.

5. *Companies are taking diversity more seriously.* Smart organizations, including some cited in the article, are addressing pay gaps; others are creating resource groups to support a range of diversity issues, and others are increasing efforts to promote a more diverse workforce.

6. *The workforce is aging*—and more older workers are remaining in the workforce for a variety of reasons including financial ones and as a way to remain engaged with the work they are doing and with their coworkers.

 **Notes to Myself**

Remember that earlier in this chapter we looked at the idea of a "preferred future"? Why not play with some possibilities that move you in the direction of your preferred future right now? Put your imagination and creativity to work, along with your knowledge of trends that we've just reviewed. Then answer the following questions:

1. **Imagine your ideal work setting.** It could be the same setting you are in now. Or it could be in a different area of library-related work (public, school, academic, special library, health care, corporate sector, information services work in an information organization, or working for yourself). Or consider a setting totally different from anything you've considered up to this point. Describe it here.

   _____

   _____

   _____

2. Describe this setting in detail as you think it might appear three to five years from now.

   _____

   _____

   _____

3. **Describe the type of work you are doing (the work you want to be doing) in your chosen setting three to five years from now.** Recall the trends you have just reviewed and incorporate the types of work activities that the trends suggest will be important.

   _____

   _____

   _____

4. **Describe the population you are serving** (the patrons, students, clients, customers, employees, etc.).

_____

_____

_____

5. **What will you offer them in services, programs, or products?** Again, consider the trends that will likely be of most importance in the future.

_____

_____

_____

Look back at your answers. You'll find that you have actually started creating a blueprint for steps you can start taking now that can move you in the direction you've just described in this activity!

## Notes

1. Seth Godin, *Linchpin: Are You Indispensable?* (New York: Penguin Group, 2010), 2.
2. Alida Draudt and Julia Rose West, *What the Foresight: Your Personal Futures Explored. Defy the Expected and Define the Preferred* (self-pub., CreateSpace, April 27, 2016).
3. Karl K. Szpunar and Kathleen B. McDermott, "Remembering the Past to Imagine the Future," *Cerebrum*, February 15, 2007, www.dana.org/Cerebrum/Default.aspx?id=39378/.
4. Ibid.
5. BusinessDictionary.com, "Backcasting," www.businessdictionary.com/definition/backcasting.html.
6. Richard A. K. Lum, *4 Steps to the Future: A Quick and Clean Guide to Creating Foresight* (Honolulu, HI: Vision Foresight Strategy, 2016).
7. Jamais Cascio, "Futures Thinking: Mapping the Possibilities, Part 2," *Fast Company*, February 12, 2010, www.fastcompany.com/1547923/futures-thinking-mapping-possibilities-part-2/.
8. Ibid.
9. American Library Association, "Trends," Center for the Future of Libraries, www.ala.org/tools/future/trends/.
10. Mozilla Foundation and Peer 2 Peer University, in collaboration with the MacArthur Foundation, "Open Badges for Lifelong Learning: Exploring an Open Badge Ecosystem to Support Skill Development and Lifelong Learning for Real Results Such as Jobs and Advancement," January 23, 2013, https://wiki.mozilla.org/images/b/b1/OpenBadges-Working-Paper_092011.pdf, quoted in Center

for the Future of Libraries, "Badging," American Library Association, www.ala.org/tools/future/trends/badging/.

11.  Mimi Ito, "Connected Learning: An Agenda for Social Change," *Huffington Post*, January 15, 2013, www.huffingtonpost.com/mimi-ito/connected-learning_b_2478940.html, quoted in Center for the Future of Libraries, "Connected Learning," American Library Association, www.ala.org/tools/future/trends/connectedlearning/.

12.  Ann Markusen and Anne Gadwa, "Creative Placemaking," National Endowment for the Arts, 2010, www.arts.gov/sites/default/files/CreativePlacemaking-Paper.pdf and Susan Silberberg, Katie Lorah, Rebecca Disbrow, and Anna Muessig, "Places in the making: How placemaking builds places and communities," MIT Department of Urban Studies and Planning, 2013, https://dusp.mit.edu/sites/dusp.mit.edu/files/attachments/project/mit-dusp-places-in-the-making.pdf, quoted in Center for the Future of Libraries, "Creative Placemaking," American Library Association, www.ala.org/tools/future/trends/creativeplacemaking/.

13.  Lynn Zubernis, "The Geek Grandpa: Leonard Nimoy's Pivotal Role in the Rise of Fandom," Raw Story, March 5, 2015, www.rawstory.com/2015/03/the-geek-grandpa-leonard-nimoys-pivotal-role-in-the-rise-of-fandom/, quoted in Center for the Future of Libraries, "Fandom," American Library Association, www.ala.org/tools/future/trends/fandom/.

14.  Barack Obama, "Remarks by the President on Economic Mobility," The White House, December 4, 2013, https://obamawhitehouse.archives.gov/the-press-office/2013/12/04/remarks-president-economic-mobility/, quoted in Center for the Future of Libraries, "Income Inequality," American Library Association, www.ala.org/tools/future/trends/incomeinequality/.

15.  Institute for Policy Studies. "Income Inequality." http://inequality.org/income-inequality/, quoted in Center for the Future of Libraries, "Income Inequality," American Library Association, www.ala.org/tools/future/trends/incomeinequality/.

16.  Daniel C. Vock, "Facing Climate Change, Cities Embrace Resiliency," *Governing*, September 2014, www.governing.com/topics/transportation-infrastructure/gov-climate-change-cities-resiliency.html, quoted in Center for the Future of Libraries, "Resilience," American Library Association, www.ala.org/tools/future/trends/resilience/.

17.  Patrick Doyle, Mitch Gelman, and Sam Gill, "Viewing the Future? Virtual Reality in Storytelling," Knight Foundation, March 13, 2016, www.knightfoundation.org/reports/vrjournalism/, quoted in Center for the Future of Libraries, "Virtual Reality," American Library Association, www.ala.org/tools/future/trends/virtualreality/.

18.  Will Oremus, "Terrifyingly Convenient," *Slate*, April 3, 2016, www.slate.com/articles/technology/cover_story/2016/04/alexa_cortana_and_siri_aren_t_novelties_anymore_they_re_our_terrifyingly.html, quoted in Center for the Future of Libraries, "Voice Control," American Library Association, www.ala.org/tools/future/trends/voicecontrol/.

19.  Dan Schwabel, "10 Workplace Trends You'll See in 2018," *Forbes*, November 1, 2017, www.forbes.com/sites/danschawbel/2017/11/01/10-workplace-trends-youll-see-in-2018/#1da3bfb84bf2/.

## CHAPTER 6

· · · · · · · · ·

# Which Opportunities Are Worth Pursuing?

W hen is *an* opportunity *the* opportunity that's right for you? How do you choose? Before you begin to explore the wide range of growth opportunities that may be available to you, you will need to have some sort of screening method in place to determine which opportunities are ones you may want to consider and which ones may not be such a good fit for you—at least not right now. Otherwise, the full range of options open to you will likely seem overwhelming, and you'll have a harder time narrowing down your choices to the ones that feel right and work best for you.

A great way to begin appraising the wide range of potential opportunities open to you is to start with reviewing the self-assessment results you got from the work you did in chapter 4 and your reflections from looking at trends and other futurist tools in chapter 5. Then, building on those valuable insights, you can combine that information with the answers to some additional questions related to the direction you want to be going. Once you've had the chance to review that final group of questions in this chapter, you'll be better able to choose growth opportunities that are best suited to getting you moving forward and have more clarity about what you want to offer to your field. It doesn't matter if you aren't crystal clear about the direction you want to be heading just yet (especially if you want to explore some new or different options in complementary fields); but it *is* important to determine what your next step will be, so you can move into action now. Once you begin screening, you'll get some momentum going, and it will be easier to make future choices about which opportunities to pursue going forward.

# Determine Your Best Opportunities

So let's start the process of determining your best potential growth opportunities. Each person's decision about which opportunities to pursue will look a bit different because each of us prioritizes differently and places a different emphasis on certain things given how we organize and want to shape our careers and our lives.

First, to give you a comprehensive picture of who you are and how you want to move forward through choosing the right opportunities to pursue, fill in answers to the questions in the two sections below. Part 1 reflects the material you looked at in chapter 5. When you're finished with part 1, move to part 2 and answer the questions by summarizing your learning from chapter 4. Though at first some questions in part 2 may look like you've already answered them earlier in the book, the questions listed here are meant to summarize and crystallize your learning about yourself.

## Part 1: Summarize Your Smarts about the Future

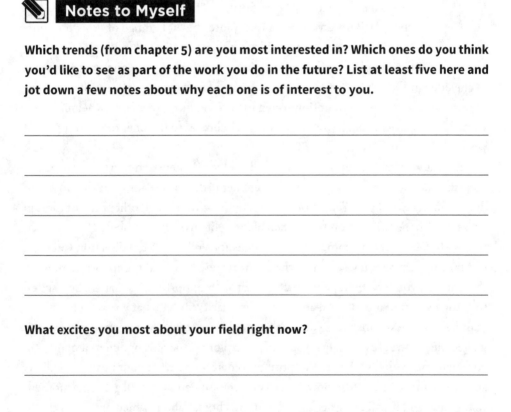

**Notes to Myself**

**Which trends (from chapter 5) are you most interested in? Which ones do you think you'd like to see as part of the work you do in the future? List at least five here and jot down a few notes about why each one is of interest to you.**

_____

_____

_____

_____

**What excites you most about your field right now?**

_____

_____

_____

**Which of the following choices, A or B, is more appealing to you right now?**

**Choice A: Growing in place (staying in the same position you hold right now or finding a similar position somewhere else *doing the same type of work*)**

OR

**Choice B: Exploring new options by taking on *a different type of position or specialization*—either at your current workplace or somewhere else**

_____

_____

_____

**Which of the following choices, A or B, is more appealing to you right now?**

**Choice A: Working within a more traditional library setting (public, school, academic, or special library) or information services setting**

OR

**Choice B: Working in a more nontraditional setting (including places like corporate, high-tech, marketing, or self-employment) where your job title may not even have the words *librarian*, *library staffer*, or *information services worker* in it**

_____

_____

_____

An important point to remember here: If you want to explore all types of opportunities (those in traditional settings as well as those in more nontraditional settings), that's OK too. Just know that, at first, the opportunities you choose to pursue may not feel as focused because you're exploring a wider range of possibilities. So you'll want to observe carefully and keep good notes to get a feel for what you learned and liked/didn't like for each opportunity you pursue.

**What is your vision of what or how you'd like to contribute to your field right now?**

_____

_____

_____

**What do you think are the most important challenges in your field that really need to be addressed at this time?**

_____

_____

_____

**How would you like to help address them?**

_____

_____

_____

**What do you think are the most fascinating opportunities opening up in your field now and what is your guess about the ones that may appear five years from now?**

_____

_____

_____

**How would you like to be a part of these opportunities?**

_____

_____

_____

**How would you describe your available time right now in terms of your ability to participate in activities beyond those of your regular workday?** (Of course, we're all busy—with work, school, family, community commitments, etc.) This question asks if you would be able to make some time available beyond your workday during weekends, evenings, lunch hours—even fifteen or thirty minutes, or more time if needed—if making the time available would involve you in something you feel very committed to or are passionate about. There is no wrong answer here. You're just clarifying what's possible for you right now.

_____

_____

_____

**How much value do you place on your professional growth at this time?** (This isn't a question about judging your commitment to your field—it simply reflects how much you are able, at the present time, to prioritize your professional growth and learning.)

_____

_____

_____

**What is the way you most enjoy participating in learning activities? Do you prefer to join with others? Take on a challenge alone? Learn by reading and reflecting? Learn by diving in and doing?**

_____

_____

_____

## Part 2: Summarize Your Smarts about You

You may want to refer back to the answers you gave in the self-assessment section of chapter 4 to help you complete this section.

List the knowledge that you possess right now that you feel is most relevant, up-to-date, and valuable.

_____

_____

_____

List three *new* areas of knowledge that you'd like to learn about.

_____

_____

_____

What three areas of knowledge (in your field) do you believe will be the most important to have in the next five years?

_____

_____

_____

Look at your answers to the previous three questions. List one area of knowledge that you are most interested in (regardless of whether or not you possess that knowledge right now).

_____

_____

**List your top five skills (whether you are using them as much as you'd like to or not).**

1. _____

2. _____

3. _____

4. _____

5. _____

**List the top three to five skills you'd like to use more.**

1. _____

2. _____

3. _____

4. _____

5. _____

**List three to five areas that represent new skills you haven't yet mastered but you'd like to learn.**

1. _____

2. _____

3. _____

4. _____

5. _____

**List your top five prioritized values.**

1. _____

2. _____

3. _____

4. _____

5. _____

**What strengths do you most enjoy using?**

1. _____

2. _____

3. _____

4. _____

5. _____

**When you consider your own feelings about risk-taking, under which conditions do you think you would be willing to take some risk in pursuing a growth opportunity?**

1. _____

2. _____

3. _____

4. _____

5. _____

**When you think about your professional life going forward, what do you aspire to? How about in your life overall?**

1. _____

2. _____

3. _____

4. _____

5. _____

**Looking back at chapter 4, what unique perspective do you have that makes you particularly good at your work?**

_____

_____

_____

**In what situations do you get to demonstrate your unique perspective the most?**

_____

_____

_____

**What would you like to be known as the "go-to" person for?**

_____

_____

_____

**What is the cutting edge you'd like to be on?**

_____

_____

_____

**Consider the organization you work in and your area of specialization. Do you know what will likely be the most important issue or challenge for your organization and for your specialization over the next year?**

_____

_____

_____

**What are the key projects that your organization is focusing on right now? Do they have a vision they are working toward? What is it?**

_____

_____

_____

**If you're not employed right now, do some basic research on the kind of setting you would like to work in (e.g., public libraries). Consider what you believe will be most important to them.**

_____

_____

_____

||||||||||||||||||||||||||||||||||||||||||||||||||||||||||||||||||||||||||||||||||||||||||

Okay, time out. Take a break—get up and stretch—listen to your favorite music. Do anything that lets you unwind from all the hard work you just did. You may want to check out some library-related cartoons at cartoonstock.com/sitesearch.asp (type "libraries" into the search box) and find a couple that make you smile.[1]

Once you've cleared your head a bit and feel ready to start putting all of these puzzle pieces together, come on back and let's get started.

What you've just done is put together a great picture of who you are, what you offer, and how you'd like to go about moving your career forward. That is a huge accomplishment. And it will be very useful as you choose growth opportunities that you want to pursue.

## What You Know and What This Means

Let's summarize what you've accomplished.

**What you know:** You now have a grasp of the most important *knowledge* you possess right now—and the knowledge you want to pick up, beyond what you already know.

**What this means:** Now you should also have a sense about whether you are primarily interested in deepening your current knowledge bank or gaining additional expertise and breadth by pursuing other areas of knowledge you've not yet acquired.

||||||||||||||||||||||||||||||||||||||||||||||||||||||||||||||||||||||||||||||||||||||||||

**What you know:** You have done enough reflecting and research to have a feel for the *knowledge that will be most important* (in your field) going forward.

**What this means:** You can target growth opportunities that focus on venues where you can gain knowledge in specific areas that will be valued in your current and future workplace.

||||||||||||||||||||||||||||||||||||||||||||||||||||||||||||||||||||||||||||||||||||||||||

**What you know:** You know the skills in which you shine.

**What this means:** You can look for opportunities where your skill set will
be valued, letting you "cash in" on the skills you already know well. This
means that pursuing opportunities that require or value a particular set
of skills that you already have can be an advantage because you're not
"starting from scratch."

Here is an example of a library professional doing just that: Aidy Weeks is a librarian
working at a medical library that is part of a health care system in central Florida.
Weeks has an amazing range of skills and role responsibilities too! Included in her skill
set is her skill in helping patients who come into one of the libraries on her health care
campus looking for information related to their medical condition. Weeks's skill set
also includes fluency in Spanish. Recently, her health care system decided to expand
their services to the Spanish-speaking population near their hospital system. Weeks
was asked to be a part of this effort by agreeing to be interviewed in Spanish for radio
and television spots to explain the full range of services to area residents. Her skill in
being able to answer patient questions related to finding relevant information on their
medical condition, and her bilingual fluency made her a great fit for this opportunity.[2]

||||||||||||||||||||||||||||||||||||||||||||||||||||||||||||||||||||||||||||||||||||||||||||||||

**What you know:** You now have an accurate read on the *skills* you want to
use more, those you may want to pick up from scratch, and those you'd
rather not use (at least not as much as you have in the past).

**What this means:** You can look for and identify opportunities that let you
learn the new skills you're interested in acquiring and avoid the opportunities where you would simply be recycling those skills that you'd
prefer to leave behind.

For example, I recently learned about the career story of Keith, an adjunct instructor
(in LIS) who loved being a problem solver. Keith loved communications too. And in
his free time, he participated in a community theater group. Low on his list of motivated skills were those that didn't give him a chance to be very creative and ones in which
he needed to follow rather strict guidelines. Keith could certainly do these things, follow set routines, adhere to tight guidelines—they just weren't the favorite parts of his
job. In choosing a growth opportunity for himself, he decided that serving on committees in which he would need to be the keeper of the budget, assist in putting policies into place, or do similar administrative work probably wouldn't get him excited.
But working with another colleague to develop skits for LIS students that focused on
challenges librarians have with patrons around certain communication issues got him

really excited. And the chance to teach the students some problem-solving skills also excited him. Such an opportunity let Keith use the skills he enjoyed and stretched his "theatrical" and communication skills that he wanted to hone. And it allowed him to challenge himself to take his problem-solving skills and apply them in new ways as he helped librarians-to-be figure out ways to deal with unhappy patrons.

||||||||||||||||||||||||||||||||||||||||||||||||||||||||||||||||||||||||||||||||||||||

**What you know:** You know the trends that will be most important in your field and in the workplace in the days ahead and the potential impact of these trends on your field and your career.

**What this means:** You are in a great position to identify opportunities (or create them) to respond to the challenges and needs of your employer, even before they become challenges. And if you're self-employed, you will be able to best assist those you serve by helping them get ahead of the changes that these trends will bring.

||||||||||||||||||||||||||||||||||||||||||||||||||||||||||||||||||||||||||||||||||||||

**What you know:** You have more information about the direction you may want to go in the future—either deepening or broadening (or both!) your knowledge and skill sets. You've started to think through the kind of work setting you prefer going forward.

**What this means:** You'll be better able to identify those opportunities that best help you deepen your current area of interest or specialization, versus those opportunities that let you take on opportunities that broaden and stretch what you already know.

||||||||||||||||||||||||||||||||||||||||||||||||||||||||||||||||||||||||||||||||||||||

**What you know:** You have begun to get a sense of whether you want to stay in the same type of setting you're in now, or whether you're hungry for a new type of work setting and new types of responsibilities.

**What this means:** This information will steer you toward opportunities to grow right where you are or consider ways you can pursue new areas of learning and new adventures.

||||||||||||||||||||||||||||||||||||||||||||||||||||||||||||||||||||||||||||||||||||||||||||||||||||

**What you know:** You have discovered the ways you wish to contribute to your field, your specialization, or your position.

**What this means:** It's important to realize that you want to contribute—but even more important to know *what* it is that you want to contribute and *how* you want to do so. This information will help you make sound choices about the opportunities that will let you do that.

||||||||||||||||||||||||||||||||||||||||||||||||||||||||||||||||||||||||||||||||||||||||||||||||||||

**What you know:** You're much more aware of the challenges facing your field, your position, and your organization now and in the near future.

**What this means:** You can choose growth opportunities that will let you partner with others (colleagues, coworkers, leaders, associations) to work to resolve these challenges.

||||||||||||||||||||||||||||||||||||||||||||||||||||||||||||||||||||||||||||||||||||||||||||||||||||

**What you know:** You should be clearer now about the difference you want to make—you probably had some sense of this before, but now you may be able to better articulate that.

**What this means:** You can discern those opportunities that will give you the chance to make a difference in the way that you truly want to. And you can avoid those opportunities that don't make room for that.

||||||||||||||||||||||||||||||||||||||||||||||||||||||||||||||||||||||||||||||||||||||||||||||||||||

**What you know:** You've taken the time to appraise and reflect on how much time, energy, and effort you can give to your own professional development right now.

**What this means:** This is crucial information! Rather than let yourself get overwhelmed or burned out, you can selectively choose those opportunities that fit into your life right now. And you can scale any opportunities you choose so that they are do-able, and enjoyable for you.

||||||||||||||||||||||||||||||||||||||||||||||||||||||||||||||||||||||||||||||||

**What you know:** You have a clearer picture of the core *values* that matter the most to you right now.

**What this means:** You can choose opportunities in line with your values and preferences. For instance, if you value independence, novelty, and creativity, then you may be most interested in growth opportunities that let you "own" a project, where you can design and implement a program or a service from scratch. Or you may be more interested in taking on shorter-term learning opportunities that involve a team effort but let you go off on your own to do some of the work and return to your group to touch base and set the agenda for going forward to work on a different piece of the shared challenge.

||||||||||||||||||||||||||||||||||||||||||||||||||||||||||||||||||||||||||||||||

**What you know:** You know what it means to demonstrate your very best. You know what strengths allow you to shine—and you love the times when you can use your unique *strengths*.

**What this means:** You may want to look for opportunities that build on these strengths and let you really experience working at your own peak performance level.

||||||||||||||||||||||||||||||||||||||||||||||||||||||||||||||||||||||||||||||||

**What you know:** You know your own tolerance level when it comes to taking reasonable *risks*.

**What this means:** Everyone differs on what they consider to be a "risk." It isn't a matter of needing to take risks that make you anxious or highly uncomfortable. It's more a matter of determining when and under what circumstances you would be willing to take a risk; and now that you have assessed your own comfort level with risk-taking, you're much more likely to choose opportunities that push you just enough to grow beyond your current comfort zone and, in the process, expand your possibilities.

||||||||||||||||||||||||||||||||||||||||||||||||||||||||||||||||||||||||||||||||||||||

**What you know:** You've either reaffirmed, gotten back in touch with, or determined new professional *aspirations* for yourself. You've revisited old dreams or shaped new dreams and hopes for what your life would look like if you were to contribute your best and brightest self to the work you do—or want to do going forward.

**What this means:** Clarity about your aspirations means you will much more easily choose growth opportunities that take you in the direction that feels right for you now. And you'll be less likely to pursue opportunities just for the sake of "doing something."

||||||||||||||||||||||||||||||||||||||||||||||||||||||||||||||||||||||||||||||||||||||

Now that you have compiled a comprehensive picture of who you are, what you can bring to the table, and where you'd like to be heading (generally), here are some criteria to consider as you review and choose different growth opportunities.

# Three Signs of a Growth Opportunity Worth Pursuing

A great way to identify the best opportunities for you to pursue is to put each one through the 3P filter. The 3P filter helps you determine if an opportunity is (1) personally meaningful, (2) positively challenging, and (3) professionally on-target. Read on to learn more about each category.

## Personally Meaningful

The growth opportunities you choose need to be ones you're drawn to—in other words, they should matter to you. In the next chapter, you're going to see a huge array of opportunities. Some of them will appeal, some won't. That's good—otherwise you'd have a difficult time choosing among them. Look back at what you wrote earlier about your top values. Look also at how you responded to the question about how you want to make a difference in your field and what gives meaning to your work. Your answers to these questions should offer some strong hints about which opportunities resonate with what matters most to you as you consider how you want to grow your career.

Why is it so important to pursue opportunities that offer meaning and purpose? At first glance, this question seems like it has an obvious answer: because when something moves us, we feel a sense of purpose and meaning and we're more committed to it. We're also more likely to find that cause, issue, or opportunity more satisfying and important to us. Of course, that makes sense.

But there's even more proof on the benefits of pursuing "personally meaningful" opportunities. Annie McKee, a senior fellow at the University of Pennsylvania Graduate School of Education, has researched this topic and believes that seeking meaning is one of the top three activities that foster happiness in our work. Here's what she says:

> We must actively seek meaning and purpose in our day-to-day activities.... Purpose is a powerful driver of workplace happiness. Yet too often we fail to tap this wellspring of motivation.... It's easy to lose sight of what we value and ignore the aspects of work that matter to us.... And if that happens, disengagement is just around the corner. In the absence of meaning, we have no reason to give our all.
>
> Each of us finds meaning and purpose in work differently, but in my experience with people from all over the globe and in all professions, I've seen some similarities: We want to fight for a cause we care about. We want to create and innovate. We want to fix problems and improve our workplaces. We want to learn and grow.[3]

What is the main message we can take away from McKee's words? Meaning gives shape and form to our lives. So why not choose to pursue those growth opportunities that connect you to those ideas, ideals, causes, and issues that you most value?

## Positively Challenging

Choosing to pursue an opportunity that you could do so easily you wouldn't even have to think about it isn't really an opportunity. It's simply performing a rote task that doesn't move you forward at all. Though it's easy, it isn't challenging. There isn't any growth involved. If you find yourself veering toward opportunities that look easy and quick to accomplish, hold off a minute. Consider why you're pursuing growth opportunities in the first place—it's not to fulfill somebody else's to-do list. It isn't so you can fill in a line on an upcoming performance review. You have chosen to pursue growth opportunities because you want to stretch yourself, grow your career, and expand your professional possibilities. To stretch, you need to challenge yourself—enough to feel the stretch but not so much that you're overwhelmed and demotivated.

## Professionally On-Target

Check back to your responses to the questions about what is most important to your organization in the coming year. Once you have done that and reviewed the range of opportunities listed in the next chapter, begin to jot down ideas for the growth opportunities you're thinking of pursuing. Then ask yourself if the opportunities you are interested in also align with the goals and vision of your organization. I don't mean to suggest that all the growth opportunities you pursue have to fall neatly in line with where your organization wants to go. But it is worthwhile to ask yourself which of the opportunities you choose will also benefit your organization.

For example, choosing to become better at public speaking may be on your list of opportunities you want to pursue because you hope to eventually do more outreach work in your community to better explain the services your library offers. That may well be in line with your organization's vision of partnering with community to a greater extent. On the other hand, you may want to pursue an opportunity to take a course that will increase your knowledge of a certain type of technology. Technology may not be one of the key duties in your current role—and further, the particular technology you want to learn more about may not be one that's in use in your workplace right now and not likely to be in the near future. So it might not fit into the plan your organization has for the coming year—especially when it comes to what your work contributes to the organization as a whole. That opportunity may be high on your list—nothing wrong with that—but don't expect that your organization will necessarily cover the cost of that course or agree to let you have time off to take that course. And that's OK too. This is *your* plan for *your* growth. Just be sure to factor in some hurdles you may have to deal with on your journey toward pursuing your chosen opportunities. You may be pursuing these without a lot of support from your employer. You would do well to consider balancing the opportunities on your "want-to-do" list so that you have some that benefit your organization's goals along with those that are of interest primarily to you.

## Other Criteria to Consider

### Is the Time Right?

Deciding whether or not to pursue opportunities does not have to be a yes/no decision. A better way to approach the question is to ask: Is the timing right to pursue *this* specific opportunity *right now?* Look back at your responses to questions in the previous chapter that asked about the time and energy you have available right now. Those questions were meant to prompt you to think about how much time you actually have to go after opportunities, given what else is on your plate right now. Of course, most opportunities will require time and effort from you, but each will demand a different amount of time—pursuing opportunities is not about stressing yourself out. It's about finding joy and satisfaction in growing. It may help for you to consider your overall strategy for career growth (coming up in chapter 8) and then look at the individual opportunity you're thinking about pursuing. Does this opportunity fit into your growth strategy? Some opportunities may not fit, but you'd still like to pursue them for the sheer enjoyment of new learning or for the fun factor—that's OK too. Just remember that they will take up your time and energy. If the opportunity does fit into your strategy, consider other time-related factors too. Is the opportunity you're considering one that is shorter-term in duration? Or will pursuing and accomplishing it take a longer period to complete? Will it require time away from work over an extended time period? Is it an opportunity that can be pursued through on-the-job training that can be woven into your workday?

## Which Way Are You Leaning?

Are you leaning toward it? Or are you approaching it kicking and screaming? When approaching opportunities, this can be a tough one. Most of us are quite used to choosing what we think we "should" choose—the option that would be good for us, the one that would make the most sense. But as we all know from previous experiences, that choice sometimes works and sometimes doesn't. If you find that you're trying to talk yourself into pursuing an opportunity, consider it a possible red flag. Once we commit to going after an opportunity that does not hold our interest or hold much meaning, it's likely we won't give 100 percent to it—and we may not finish it either. This is the time to choose opportunities we can lean into—not shrink back from our commitment to giving it our all.

## What's the Attraction?

When deciding on which new skill you would like to develop, you might follow the advice of author Jon Acuff, who asks, "What's one new skill we want to learn? There are two easy ways to pick one: by necessity or curiosity."[4]

You can consider your growth strategy (you'll shape it in chapter 8)—or you can set it aside in making your choice. If you're feeling some urgency because developing a new skill or acquiring new knowledge will make the difference between keeping you employable, getting you that raise, or fulfilling a requirement that will position you for other opportunities in the near future versus *not* having any of these important things happen, then the acquisition of that skill or new knowledge may be more of a necessity and, thus, take priority over other opportunities.

If, however, you've had a long-standing interest in learning more about some specific topic, area, or skill set, then the sheer joy or desire to find out more may win out. If *this* is the filter you're using, then your inquisitiveness may take priority. Here's a short quiz that may help you decide.

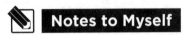

## Notes to Myself

**Consider these questions to appraise your opportunities.**[5]

1. What might this opportunity give you that you don't have now?

   _____

2. Will it help you grow in new ways or merely give you one more variation of what you already know?

   _____

3. Does it point you in the direction you want to be heading?

   _____

4. Does it pique your curiosity about something you haven't previously considered?

   _____

5. What are the trade-offs if you take this opportunity? What will you gain? What will you have to sacrifice? Are the trade-offs worth it?

   _____

   _____

6. If you don't grab this opportunity, what will you potentially miss?

   _____

   _____

7. If this opportunity doesn't seem to be worthwhile, based on how you've answered the questions so far, why are you drawn to it?

_____

_____

Opportunities—the new definition of career smarts—are all around you. Make certain you choose the very best ones for you!

## Notes

1. Cartoonstock.com, "Libraries," www.cartoonstock.com/sitesearch.asp?categories=All+Categories& artists=All+Artists&mainArchive=mainArchive&newsCartoon=newsCartoon&vintage=vintage& ANDkeyword=libraries&searchBoxButton=SEARCH/.
2. Aidy Weeks, phone interview with the author, December 2017.
3. Annie McKee, "Happiness Traps," *Harvard Business Review*, September–October 2017, https://hbr.org/2017/09/happiness-traps/.
4. Jon Acuff, *Do Over: Make Today the First Day of Your New Career* (New York: Penguin, 2017), 124.
5. Caitlin Williams, *Successful Woman's Guide to Working Smart: 10 Strengths That Matter Most* (Palo Alto, CA: Davies-Black, 2001), 181.

CHAPTER 7
· · · · · · · · ·

# Growth Opportunities
# Are Everywhere!

I hope that by now you're beginning to embrace the idea that opportunities can show up just about anywhere—often right in front of you! You just need to know how and where to look. The best way to do that? By knowing an opportunity when you see one and by going about your life with an opportunity-minded perspective. At this point, you may be thinking, *And just how do I do that?* Not to worry—that's where we're going next. To spot opportunities, it's a good idea to pay attention to how you're defining "opportunity" for yourself in the first place. After you're clear on your own definition of opportunity, you'll also want to make certain that you nurture an opportunity-minded perspective as you go about your day-to-day life. An opportunity-minded perspective simply means that you don't live your life on "stand-by," waiting to be told what to do or waiting for the approval of someone else before you move forward with any action or any problem-solving thinking on your part. You keep your eyes and ears open for possibilities!

## Your Definition of *Opportunity* and *Opportunity-Mindedness*

Before you go any further in this chapter, take a few moments now to get clear on your own definitions of *opportunity* and *opportunity-mindedness*. Earlier in this book, I described an opportunity, per Dictionary.com, as "an appropriate or favorable time or occasion, a situation or condition favorable for attainment of a goal, or a good position, chance or prospect, as for success."[1] I also noted that an opportunity can be represented by a particular moment, or a set of circumstances that presents itself. Or it can even be a change in one's thinking or belief that offers a different perspective.

While that is how *this* book describes an opportunity, it's important that you are clear on *your* definition of it to maximize your own options for career growth. Fill in the lines below with your definition of "an opportunity," including your own criteria for what makes something an opportunity to you.

### 🖉 Notes to Myself

_____

_____

_____

_____

As you look at what you've just written, consider these questions:

- Is your definition and criteria sufficiently broad (meaning you haven't made it so narrow that few possibilities you come across would qualify as opportunities in your eyes)?

- Does your definition and criteria take into account possibilities and activities in which you don't necessarily know whether or not they will turn out successfully? In other words, are you willing to take a risk (even a small one) by pursuing an opportunity in which you can't guarantee the outcome ahead of time?

- Does your definition and criteria include possibilities or actions that won't necessarily result in accolades from your boss, a promotion, or even recognition from others? Is an opportunity only an opportunity if you get praise or compensation for pursuing it? Or is your interest in pursuing the opportunity greater than the kudos you hope to get for pursuing it?

- Last, does your definition of *opportunity* mean pursuing only those possibilities that are easy to stick with and don't challenge you too much?

Or does it reflect your belief that you have what it takes to stay motivated through the inevitable ups and downs of pursuing something that is likely to take you out of your comfort zone?

When it comes to defining opportunities for yourself, the more open and flexible you can be, the more options you'll notice to explore.

Next question: Just how opportunity-minded are you? When a coworker complains that a particular system has just never worked well, do you automatically commiserate, agree that it's a problem, and throw up your hands in resignation? Or do you wonder how the system could be improved so that it *would* work—and begin to figure out just how that could be done?

When you notice a gap in the outreach services your organization provides, do you mention it to your boss and leave it at that? Or do you mention it to your boss *and* come prepared with a couple ideas for closing the gap that your boss might be interested in hearing about?

When you go to a conference and attend a presentation on a particular piece of technology that really impresses you, do you silently wish you had that technology in your organization (and then sigh in frustration) and leave it at that? Or do you go back to your workplace, consider how that technology you just learned about might make a real difference for those you serve, research it, and make a business case to your boss for adopting it (or find some other technology that may cost less, be more budget-friendly, and still benefit those you serve)?

When you are opportunity-minded, you may see a problem as a challenge to be solved or at least as a curiosity that gets you thinking about alternatives that may help. Opportunity-minded professionals are always curious—it's not that they spend every available moment looking to grab on to something they hear about. They are discerning about possibilities they hear about or challenges they notice.

 **Notes to Myself**

How about you? How would you rate yourself on the Opportunity-Minded Scale on the next page? Circle the number that best represents your own opportunity-mindedness.

**Figure 7.1.** Opportunity-Minded Scale

| 0 | 3 | 5 | 7 | 9 |
|---|---|---|---|---|
| Opportunities just don't naturally occur to me | Every once in a while I notice an opportunity, but I don't usually do anything about it | If I notice something, I may get interested in learning more about it if I think I can easily take action on it | I often see opportunities and think about how I might do something to take action on them or capitalize on them in some way | I make a habit of being on the outlook for opportunities and how I could capitalize on them or make a difference by taking action |

How did you score yourself here? There is no "correct" answer. Be aware, though, that the higher you scored yourself, the more options you'll see. And if you scored yourself low, reflect on the reasons you did so. Are there things holding you back? Perhaps concerns over taking risks, the reluctance to try new things, or feelings of being overwhelmed may represent some obstacles for you. If that's the case, recognize that such feelings may be true right now because of life circumstances. If so, I still encourage you to look over the list of opportunities in this chapter and see if you can find a few that you could scale to a level that would make them do-able and interesting for you. Remember, there are dozens of ways you can grow. Shape your opportunities to fit for what is possible for you right now. Later on, you may be able to incorporate other opportunities into your daily life. Be patient with yourself.

Let's use these ideas of a broad definition of opportunity and the art of being opportunity-minded to get you going in the best possible direction.

If you accept the idea (*and I hope you do!*) that growth and learning opportunities are virtually everywhere, then you'll have an appreciation for just how many options are potentially open to you. With that large number of options in mind, it's a good idea to consider how best to organize and review the range of possibilities.

## Categorizing the Range of Opportunities

This next section is grouped into categories that suggest different possibilities that may be of interest to you. You'll see that the opportunities are listed under category headings: "The What" (listing different types of opportunities themselves), "The Where" (listing places where opportunities might be found), "The How" (listing different ways you might pursue the opportunities), and the last category—with the somewhat unusual heading of "If You . . ." (describing different circumstances that you may find yourself in at the present time, where certain obstacles may make it more challenging to pursue opportunities).

The placement of opportunities under a particular category is somewhat arbitrary, as there may be instances where an opportunity could just as easily be found in another category. Feel free to add to this list any other opportunities you have in mind. You're likely to see several opportunities that you're already aware of, as well as ones that you may not have thought about before. Either way, I invite you to look at each opportunity with "new eyes" as you consider how each particular one may help you grow right now. For instance, you may see one that suggests you sign up for a webinar. You may think, *That's not a new idea. I've attended dozens of webinars before!* That may be true, but this time around, think about how you want to grow, the venues that can help you do that (like webinars), and which specific webinars—sponsored by which groups—might offer the perfect stand-alone or ongoing series of webinars on a particular topic that would nicely move you forward right now. Don't assume a "been there, done that" attitude—instead, dig deeper to see if a specific opportunity might be useful to you right now. You'll also notice that some opportunities are repeated in different categories. That is because similar types of opportunities can be found in multiple places.

It's probably a good idea to pause before you begin going through this list to recall the ways you have determined that you want to grow right now. Look back at notes you took in earlier chapters. You'll see a lot of hints in your notes that may help you decide on specific opportunities in the list that follows. Don't worry about choosing certain ones right now as you first look through this list. You'll get suggestions for how to choose your best opportunities in the next chapter.

|||||||||||||||||||||||||||||||||||||||||||||||||||||||||||||||||||||||||||||||||||||||||

## The What

The list that follows gives an overview of the wide variety of opportunities that are potentially open to you. The list is meant to give you a robust representation of opportunities, though it doesn't include every possible opportunity—new ones are created each day and many opportunities are unique, fashioned by an individual to pursue a specific activity that is unique to that person. Still, this list should get you thinking. Be sure to add your own ideas about opportunities you could go after. You'll notice that I use the words *growth opportunity* and *learning opportunity* interchangeably through the next section. I do this because I believe that each growth opportunity also presents the chance to learn something new.

### *Attend Conferences (Local, Regional, National, International)*

Of course, you already know the value of attending a conference. But what's most important here is to look at conference attendance through the lens of a *potential learning opportunity.* Sure, you can network, pick up an idea or two, find some new resources—all of that can be helpful. But you need to be more focused to maximize the benefits of attending. Before you go, think about what you've learned about yourself—and the current and future needs of your workplace and your field that you explored so far in this book. Then choose the sessions you want to attend as they relate to that learning and to your interests and curiosities. Also consider minigoals for what you want to get from each session. Always consider what you can do with your new learning when you're back at your workplace.

### *Attend Workshops*

The ideas here are similar to the ones mentioned in the aforementioned "attend conferences" opportunity. But here are a couple more things to consider: Workshops are generally more focused, often on some particular skills or some specific new knowledge that will help you in your work. To make the most of this opportunity, consider how you can demonstrate what you've learned back at your workplace. Or how you can immediately apply it to some aspect of your work.

### *Be a Mentor*

If this is an opportunity you're interested in, you can find dozens of great resources to give you more details on how to mentor well. Mentoring is listed here as a learning opportunity because of its focus on helping you develop others while you are also developing yourself. If leadership is an area you are interested in, check out this opportunity. You may have a formal mentoring program at your workplace that you can participate in. If that's not the case, don't let that stop you. You can informally mentor, or you can do it through associations or others groups you belong to. Let others know of your interest and then determine how you can best make this a learning opportunity for you (as well as the person you mentor).

### *Be Mentored*

Is there an area you could really use some help on? Perhaps it's something that isn't covered in a class or workshop, or it isn't included in the employee manual. If you could use some assistance on things like company culture or guidelines for advancement that don't seem to be written down anywhere—anything that would help you grow your career or get past a stuck spot—consider asking someone you admire for some mentoring. Be clear about what you are looking for and think about what you might give back in return.

### Coach

The late Sir John Whitmore, a leader in coaching and leadership, noted that coaching is a way of "unlocking a person's potential to maximize his/her performance."[2] Think about the areas in which you already have some expertise or special knowledge. Could others, like someone new to the job or someone who is struggling to understand an area that you're already well-versed in, benefit from what you know? If your own interests include supporting others in their development, then coaching in an area that you know a great deal about could be a great opportunity for you (and for the person you're coaching!).

### Collaborate

There are tons of ways you can collaborate with others: research, presentations, participating in panels, facilitating workshops—the list goes on. The important thing here is that whether you're inviting someone else to collaborate with you or you are the one being asked, make certain the project is one that leads you toward your own learning interests or goals.

### Committee Membership

This particular opportunity is an easy one to see as valuable. Keep in mind the areas in which you most want to grow or enrich your career. Then select committees you think would best help you do that as well as ones where you can contribute and make a difference. Depending on your workplace setting, you may be placed on some committees that are chosen by others for you. If that's the case, ask yourself how you can turn this into an opportunity that will help you grow your career. It may be through networking, taking a lead role on a particular initiative the committee is spearheading, or writing (or contributing to) a report on a particular piece of research the committee is investigating.

### Continuing Education

Tamara Acevedo sums it up well: "Choosing librarianship as a career means choosing a lifetime of continuing education."[3] You probably already know that, but I include it here as a reminder that continuing education, itself, with its scores of possibilities, offers an amazing array of ways to pursue continuous growth and often pick up continuing education credits as well.

### Create Videos or Podcasts

Rather than watch videos or listen to podcasts presented by others, consider creating your own. The content possibilities are huge—depending on your area(s) of interest and your goals in creating them and making them available. There are also many platforms that can be used to create them. You can probably think of a dozen ways you could create a video or podcast—consider what you're most interested in or what you think would be most useful to your organization.

### Debriefs

If you and other colleagues or coworkers are all attending the same conference, make arrangements beforehand so that each person attends a different session on a different topic at the conference. Agree on a format for taking notes so that everyone will create similar notes and summaries at the sessions they attend. After the conference is over and you're all back home, schedule one or more debriefs in which you can all take turns sharing what you learned, what insights you gained, and what resources could benefit all of you.

### Fellowships

In a chapter of *Continuing Education for Librarians*, Cindy Mediavilla, a library programs consultant, writes about her experience in getting a fellowship. She notes, "In the library world, fellowships bring together experienced practitioners who engage with subject experts and each other to learn new skills. The Association for Library and Information Science Education has defined 'fellowship' as a learning opportunity designed to help experienced librarians develop a specialty or improve their management skills."[4] Would a fellowship give you the additional boost to grow your career? Research to see if this learning opportunity is a possibility for you.

### Informational Interview

You'll find more on the "how-to" of doing informational interviews in chapter 9. As a learning opportunity, consider conducting informational interviews with coworkers, colleagues, leaders, and other professionals within your field or in other fields who have information that you'd love to know. Perhaps they already have expertise in an area you'd like to learn more about (as a potential career move in the future). Or maybe you admire their leadership skills and you've just been promoted into management and would love their perspective. Maybe you're a recent grad and could really benefit from hearing how another new-to-the-field professional has made a successful transition.

### Internships

We're most familiar with internships as a component a student participates in as part of a degree program. It's in the best interests of students to get internships that will give them superior training and experience.

But internships can extend beyond the school years as well. A recent search of internships at Indeed.com, using the job titles or keywords *data analyst internship, archivist internship*, and *research internship*, all included internships that were open to graduate students, recently graduated students, or career changers. And some listed flexible work arrangements. Bottom line: don't discount internships as an option if you've already graduated.

### Job Enrichment

You may not be interested in moving to any other position, but you sure would like to get more satisfaction, joy, and an increased sense that you're making a difference in your current role. Do you know what would help you do that? Is it increasing one portion of the work you do? Delegating or decreasing other parts? (I know that option isn't always available.) Consider what will reenergize you or make you that go-to person you want to be. Then determine how you can weave that special something into the work you're already doing. That does not mean you should overwhelm yourself with more work! You may need some help from your boss on this one, but oftentimes a little tweaking of your current responsibilities can make a huge difference.

### Job Rotations

Author Halelly Azulay describes a rotation assignment:

> As the temporary assignment of an employee to a different job, usually laterally, in another role in the same organization for an agreed-upon period of time. The rotational job may be in the same team or department, in a new department in the same division … or in a different … unit or line of service altogether. This temporary new job may allow the employee to use existing skills in a different setting or may require the employee to learn a new set of skills in order to function in the new role.[5]

If you're looking to broaden your skills or learn more about different aspects of librarianship, information services, or administration, job rotations may be a great idea for you. Likewise, if you've been thinking about moving into more technical aspects of your field, this type of opportunity may help you get closer to that goal.

### Join an Association (or Join Several)

If you haven't yet joined a professional association aligned with your field or specialization, do so soon. If you're a student, you'll likely find that student rates for membership are lower, so, that's an incentive for those still in school. Once you join, become active! You'll have more opportunities to participate than you can ever imagine. Choose the ones that best fit your learning and growth goals. Also consider other associations and professional societies in areas beyond the ones that represent your industry. For instance, you may belong to ALA and the Association of College and Research Librarians, but you may also have a strong interest in technology. What about joining the Association of Technology Professionals? Research the broad range of associations and professional societies open to you.

### Leadership

If you know that leadership is a passion of yours, or even if you just want to gain some leadership skills with the intention of taking on leadership roles as you move forward in your career, why not look for an opportunity to start growing those skills now? Consider volunteering to lead a task force, committee, or new initiative. Also consider leading team meetings, planning professional events, or even taking a leadership role in your community.

### Lunch and Learn

Initiate an informal gathering that takes place regularly (lunchtime is often a convenient time for your coworkers), focused on particular topics of interest. Invite someone from inside or outside your organization to come in to talk about a topic. Or pool the group's expertise and take turns presenting on a specific topic. You could also build in reviews of books, tools, or technologies that the group is interested in. Decide on topics, format, and anything else that will help your group be a welcoming and successful initiative.

### Manage/Supervise

If management or supervising others isn't yet a part of your skill set but you would like it to be, have a conversation with your boss to check out your possibilities. Could you manage a small project? Help lead the launch of a new initiative? Supervise a small number of employees or volunteers? If you decide to take on this type of opportunity, make sure you prepare yourself for it: get coaching from your boss or someone else in management, read about the manager and supervisor role, and attend classes or workshops. In short, don't just jump into it; learn how you can do it effectively and then notice what's working well and what you need to work on.

### Network

There are hundreds (maybe thousands!) of articles, books, and possible venues for networking—no need to repeat them here. Networks offer so much in the way of colleagueship, valuable contacts, and an excellent way to stay savvy on important information that it would be foolish not to continue to grow yours. There are even resources for people who hate networking! If you're not particularly fond of networking, consider ditching the word *networking* and substituting it with a more meaningful word that works for you.

### Presentations

Presenting isn't as easy as some people may think. If you've already presented, you know this is true. There's a lot of up-front work involved. And it is this up-front work that offers you a growth opportunity. You'll need to thoroughly research and understand your topic (even if it's already familiar to you). You'll need to determine how you want to present it and what materials (such as slides, props, and handouts) you'll want to use. You will want to consider ways to make your presentation both engaging and useful to your audience. You'll want to use effective speaking techniques. There's also the need to practice. The list goes on and on. And no matter how many times you present, the preparation stage will always provide you with new opportunities to learn. This is true whether you're preparing a solo presentation, copresenting, or presenting as part of a panel.

### Represent Your Organization or the School Where You Received Your Degree

Interested in interacting with those outside your organization? Excited to share what's happening at your workplace (or at the school you graduated from)? There are many opportunities to speak to community groups about your organization or take part in alumni-sponsored events. Let the people who arrange these events, as well as your employer, know of your willingness to act as a representative.

### Returnships

Here's one you may not have considered! Described by Mark Koba, senior editor at CNBC, "a returnship is an internship-like program for experienced people who have been out of the labor force for some time."[6] Returnships are growing in several sectors of the economy. Designed to update skills or offer new ones, and either paid or unpaid, they can be a boon to midlifers who are looking to get back to work. They are also open to those who want to shift from one sector to another. There are some downsides to consider: not all returnships are paid; they don't guarantee a full-time, paid, regular position after the returnship period is over; and those engaging in returnships may end up taking their focus off of job searching for a full-time benefited position. Still, if you are looking to upgrade your skills, learn new ones, or learn about another sector, returnships may represent a great growth opportunity.

### Sabbatical

Sabbaticals represent paid or unpaid extended time away from work to dive deep into an area that you are truly fascinated with. We usually think of them as a perk of working in academia; yet they are also on the rise in nonacademic settings, such as corporate or nonprofit. Talk with your boss or colleagues and find out if this is an option for you.

### Shadowing

No, this isn't about skulking around someone you admire. But it is a great opportunity to learn by observing how others go about their work. Job shadowing (as it is often referred to) is described by career specialist Katharine Hansen in this way:

> Job-shadowing can be thought of as an expanded informational interview. Where an informational interview typically lasts about a half hour, a job-shadowing experience can be anywhere from a few hours, to a … week or more, depending on what you can mutually arrange with the person you've chosen to shadow.… During your job-shadow experience, you follow the professional you're shadowing through his or her work day. You observe the rigors of the job … and ask lots of questions.[7]

While job shadowing is often thought of as an activity for those still in school (and it *is* a good one for them), it is also a way to learn more about different aspects of librarianship and information services that you are curious about. Though this type of shadowing isn't formalized in a work setting, you can certainly ask about how you might do it at your workplace or even in a different workplace. Just be ready to make a strong case for why you want to do it and what you hope to learn from it, and be sure to inquire about the unspoken rules in certain workplaces that would either make this a learning opportunity that would work or one that just isn't feasible within that particular setting.

### Side Gigs (Also Called Side Hustles)

In a work world that often highlights the notion that we're in a "gig economy," side gigs have become the darling of the "alternative ways to make money" advice articles. While it's not my intent to show you all the ways you can bring in extra dollars, side gigs are listed here because they represent an opportunity for you to try another aspect of librarianship or information services–related work that you may not get to try in your current position. Whether it's work in archives, digital storytelling, coding, reference, or research, there are many opportunities for part-time work that you may truly enjoy. Sometimes, a setting like a gallery, museum, e-publishing site, or advocacy group may have opportunities for some limited, part-time work that will give you a chance to try something new or simply let you do work that fills your need to make a difference in a way that just isn't possible in your day job. And they can sometimes be done remotely.

### Speeches

If you are a library or information professional who has gained expertise in a particular area or specialty within your profession, there may be opportunities to speak at industry events, association meetings, and a whole range of other venues. Speeches share many similarities with giving presentations—but there are also some differences. Check with meeting planners for different organizations that might be interested in your expertise. Do they have any upcoming meetings that could use a speaker like yourself? Check event calendars for different groups (like your alum, your associations, trade shows, annual retreats, and specialized conventions—for instance, technology-related ones).

### Stretch Assignments

According to author Halelly Azulay, a stretch assignment

> is a task or project that employees perform *usually within their role, but beyond their job description,* that challenges and broadens (stretches) their current skills and capabilities. It forces employees to step beyond their comfort zones and develop new knowledge, skills, and abilities.[8]

The great part about stretch assignments is that you don't need to leave your current job or role to do them. You can identify possible ones for yourself, figure out who you need to talk with to get the ball rolling, and pay attention to what you are learning that is new and can enrich your current job once the stretch assignment is completed. Just be sure the assignment you decide on (or the one you are given by your boss) is enough of a stretch to be outside your comfort zone and offers you a challenge—but not so far outside that it overwhelms you or causes enough anxiety that you end up feeling defeated.

### Success Team

Author Barbara Sher came up with the idea of success teams several years ago—and her idea is just as relevant today, especially as a learning opportunity. In short, a success team is a group of supportive individuals who get together regularly to learn about the professional development activities of their fellow group members and provide encouragement and constructive feedback to one another.[9] Regular meetings help build momentum for everyone in the group—and membership is based on those you want to be part of your circle of supportive colleagues.

### Take on New Duties (Budgeting, Administrative Work, PR, etc.)

This opportunity can be a tricky one—you don't want to overwhelm yourself with more work than you can handle (especially since you may not get extra pay for doing so). But if you want to learn more aspects or a bigger picture of the work your organization does, you may want to ask if you can assist someone who does a different type of work than you do. But do so strategically. Be clear, when you ask for this type of assignment, that you're not stepping on anyone else's toes, and be clear too about the scope of the assignment and the timeline for taking it on—including when the assignment will end.

### Task Force Participation

According to YALSA (Young Adult Library Services Association), "a task force is an action-oriented membership group whose charge is to address specific goals, complete a specific task, or to consider a particular issue."[10] Because a task force focuses on a specific issue, participating in one is often a good way to delve deeper into a topic or issue of importance—or of high interest to you. Task forces are created to address a wide range of issues. A recent scanning of task forces within different areas of the ALA showed task forces on topics including hunger, homelessness, and poverty; the environment; and equity, diversity, and inclusion. Also keep in mind that task forces are set up inside organizations and professional societies, as well as being part of associations.

### Teach

It's not always easy to differentiate between teaching and training (the next entry), as both are elements of learning. For our purposes here, consider teaching an opportunity you would engage in through an academic setting: a school, community college, university, or credential-granting institution.

### Train

Training, as we're focusing on it here as a learning opportunity, is about providing learning to employees inside an organization. If you're up for it, training can be a fantastic opportunity to help others and learn more about a topic and yourself, as you strive to equip others with information to improve their job performances or learn a new skill.

### Tutor (or Be Tutored)

Want to learn a microskill? Better understand some aspect of a particular technology? Learn a slice of knowledge on a particular topic of interest? Why not ask a friend or colleague (who already knows what you want to learn) for some informal tutoring? Perhaps you can do a trade with that person and return the favor by giving them some mini-lessons that you are more knowledgeable about. Or let it be known that you are open to tutoring others on a particular topic.

### Vocation Vacations

Here's another opportunity that may be new to you. Are you interested in another field? Curious about what it would be like to try your hand at something entirely different? Vocation vacations are opportunities for you to do something you're secretly fascinated with (running your own book store, operating a bed and breakfast, starting your own travel agency) but aren't able or ready to commit to at the moment. There are organizations that can connect you with someone engaged in the kind of work you're interested in and make arrangements for you to spend extended time with this person at their location to learn the basics of what it takes (note: this isn't free). At the end of your experience, you'll be in a better position to know if this is something you'll want to transition to full-time, do on a part-time basis, volunteer at, or simply decide it's not for you.

### Write

The opportunities here are wide-ranging, from book reviews, blogging, grant writing, and contributions to newsletters to just about anything else you can think of that would be useful to your organization, association, school alum, or professionals in general. And don't forget about written contributions for community organizations that your organization may partner with as well.

||||||||||||||||||||||||||||||||||||||||||||||||||||||||||||||||||||||||||||||||||||||

## The Where

Consider the best places to pursue your growth opportunities. In many instances, it's natural to focus on those within your current work setting (you'll read more about that in the next section). In other instances, though, you may want to consider other locations beyond your own workplace to pursue opportunities that aren't employer-sponsored. Let's say you want to build a skill that is new for you—or one you're not particularly good at just yet but truly *want* to get good at (for example: negotiating, public speaking, team leadership)—and you'd rather have some practice at it first, before demonstrating it in your own workplace where others may be evaluating you on your performance. Dorie Clark, information professional, suggests this as a great way to invest the time you need to gain competence in areas where you want to stretch and grow but not be evaluated by those you may report to while you're building your skills.[11]

### Opportunities Inside Your Organization

Individual workers are not limited to—nor can they depend on—their organization to have all the resources and available opportunities they need to continue their growth.

However, don't automatically dismiss what your employer may offer. Individuals working inside an organization don't always take advantage of the variety of options for growth that *are* available to them. Organizations today are very aware that they need to develop their employees in order to retain them. Adding more options that allow their workers to grow is a high priority for almost every organization.

Whether you're a new employee or one who has been at your organization for a while, take the time to investigate your options. Talk to HR, check your employee guide, talk with a colleague, or ask your boss. Check to see if any of these options are available to you:

- In-house or regional training

- Ability to attend workshops, webinars, or guest presentations that your library or information organization may sponsor, cosponsor, or have access to because of the system they belong to or their partnerships with other organizations

- Mentoring

- Job rotations that would let you "trade places" with someone in another part of your organization to learn new skills or become cross-trained

- Job enrichment activities: taking on an assignment or initiating a project that could let you delve into an area that you're already interested in or one you'd like to explore with the purpose of making your role and your responsibilities more satisfying to you

- Committee or task force memberships or leadership

- The chance to represent your organization in the community

- Developing, designing, and delivering a class or training session in-house

- Shadowing someone in your organization to learn more about different facets of librarianship or information services

- Asking to be part of the launch of a new initiative

- Recruiting on behalf of the organization at local colleges and job fairs

### Opportunities Outside Your Organization

There will be times when your organization cannot offer the type of learning opportunities you want to pursue. And even if they can, it's still worthwhile to consider other venues for trying out new skills or picking up new knowledge. Sometimes, choosing to learn outside your own organization can offer you a different perspective or a larger, big-picture view of issues and challenges.

Many of the opportunities listed in the "The What" section can be found outside your own workplace, including these:

- conferences
- leadership (in groups that are not associated with your workplace)
- workshops
- success teams (with members who are not employed by your organization)
- volunteering
- association-related opportunities

### Opportunities Inside Your School (If Your Primary Role Right Now Is Student)

In my role as career coach at ALA's twice-yearly conferences, I'm often asked by students (many of whom are graduating in a few months' time) about when they should start looking for a job. My answer is always the same: yesterday! Seriously, it's really smart to be on the lookout for job opportunities *before* you graduate. The same idea holds true for pursuing learning and growth opportunities while you're still in school. Sure, you may not yet know the specific area of librarianship or information services you want to pursue—that's only natural. But what a great time and place to start exploring opportunities!

Where to start? Internships, or dual internships, like the one described by Michael Oden, an MLIS grad who completed a dual-library internship that allowed him to split his time between an academic library and a public library setting.[12] While dual-library internships may not be that easy to score, it is worth checking out the possibilities for internships in which there may be a possible partnership between public and academic libraries.

For those nearing graduation—especially if you're interested in looking more closely at working in academia—how about fellowships? To find out more about fellowships, you'll need to do some research (luckily, a talent you already have!).

What about work-study or part-time positions outside the university where you are getting your degree? Or what about nonprofits, library-related associations, and online entities that are looking for someone with the skills you're learning right now? Many of these places advertise remote opportunities that can be done on a part-time, virtual, and flexible basis. Don't forget that faculty members in universities often seek help in researching topics they want to write about—your research skills could be just what they are looking for—and it gives you more experience in researching all sorts of topics that may spark an interest in you.

## The How

The ways you choose to pursue your opportunities are wide-ranging, including (but not limited to) these:

### Classes

Consider those you could take online, in person, or in a hybrid format that combines both online and in-person format.

### Certifications

Depending on your area of interest and the expertise you wish to develop, there are several types of certifications you can choose. Check with associations and LIS academic programs to learn more.

### Formal/Already Set-Up Programs

Some venues including regularly scheduled retreats, programs like ALA's Emerging Leaders Program, or formal mentoring programs focus on an established program that you can join and learn along with a cohort of your peers.

### Microlearning

You may already be familiar with this term, defined by writer Asha Pandey as "a short, focused learning nugget (often 3–5 minutes long or shorter) that is designed to meet a specific learning outcome.... Typically designed and delivered in rich media formats, it is a learner-centric approach that provides just-in-time training."[13] Consider your learning goals and then determine how this approach to growth opportunities might work for you.

### Self-Directed (More Informal) Learning

Consider all the times you pick up a book or check out a YouTube video because you want to do or learn something on your own, at your own convenience. Self-directed learning is the ultimate DIY activity. You're not relying on your organization or any outside agency for resources or approval. You "sign yourself up" for this opportunity. And it's your own motivation that gets you through it.

You do the choosing, you set up the schedule for learning (mostly), and you figure out how long you're going to be at it. Some activities you might include here are

- reading a book or article(s) or watching a video/listening to a podcast,
- attending a lecture/presentation, or
- participating in a webinar (or a series of them).

If you're interested in pursuing self-directed opportunities, it's important to have your learning goal in mind, first, and then choose one or more opportunities that will get you closer to that learning goal. The upside of self-directed opportunities is that you're free to proceed on your own (with the exception of scheduled times for events you'll be signing up to watch or listen to). The downside—at least a caution to watch out for—is that since you're on your own, you don't need to report back to anyone, turn in any assignments (usually), or even let someone else know you're doing them. All the more reason to have goal(s) you set for yourself before you begin that particular activity. Also consider what you will do after you complete the activity. How will you put your new learning to use? Simply reading a book and then returning it to the library isn't enough. Always remember to ask yourself what you've learned after finishing your self-directed learning project that you didn't know beforehand and what that means for your career growth.

### Volunteer Opportunities

Volunteering, according to author Halelly Azulay, involves

> providing your knowledge, skills, and abilities, as well as your time and energy. . . . Employees who take on volunteer roles are able to build new skills and practice existing skills in a different setting from their day-to-day jobs.[14]

Volunteering is equally valuable for grad students, people temporarily unemployed, those who are self-employed, and those transitioning to retirement. Volunteering offers an excellent opportunity to learn more about an area you're interested in or sharpen skills you already have. In some ways, the pressure is off (or at least it's less) because, as a volunteer, it's usually easier to ask questions, not feel you have to get it right each time, and not feel you're being observed and evaluated by the people you work with each day. At the same time, you're expanding your network, learning that different places go about their work differently, and getting a bigger view of the world.

Still, make sure the volunteer opportunity moves you closer to a specific learning goal you have and that the volunteer match is a good one for you.

||||||||||||||||||||||||||||||||||||||||||||||||||||||||||||||||||||||||||||||||||||||||||||||||

## If You . . .

There may be some times when you want to grow in a specialized area. Or your wish to grow may be hampered by some obstacle(s) that get you stuck in your ability to proceed. With such circumstances in mind, this next section, "If You . . ." tries to address many of these situations.

### *If You Want to Go Broader Than Your Current Skill Set or Role*

Here's an interesting way to think about broadening your knowledge about other areas that either complement librarianship or information services or go beyond it. Let's say you have interest or curiosity in a particular area. You could experiment by adapting a model created by author Sally Power in her book *The Mid-Career Success Guide.* Though Power's book focuses on helping midlife professionals identify possible career options for themselves, her Work Arena Model[15] can be adapted to help you identify possible opportunities you may want to try out to learn more about different fields. Perhaps you've been curious about the work of professionals employed in other sectors who do work that complements or supports the work done in library-related or information-related organizations. For example, you may wonder, *What would it be like to be a rep for a book publisher or a writer for a nonprofit organization?* If that's the case for you, read on to learn more about her model and how you might use it.

Look at her Work Arena Model in figure 7.2. Power suggests that there is an abundance of opportunities available if we take into account all the different people, organizations, and industries that support an individual's work. For example, let's assume for the moment that you are a public librarian. Try this: put your job title "public librarian" into the center of her model (the star-shaped "burst," as she refers to it),

**Figure 7.2.** Work Arena Model

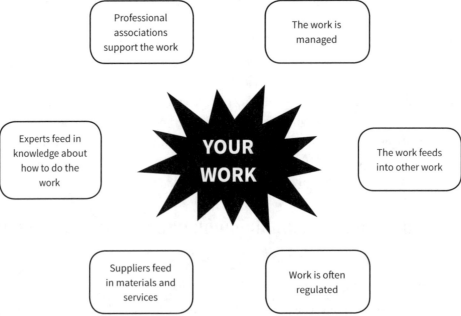

Reprinted with permission of Copyright Clearance Center, Inc., from *The Mid-Career Success Guide* by Sally J. Power (Praeger, 2006).

and then consider all the people, organizations, and industries that complement, support, or somehow are connected with your role as a public librarian. When you do that, you'll find there are dozens of entities involved. Look at her model, and you'll see how she's labeled these different entities, though you could come up with other entities that support you in your role (e.g., your role as an archivist, content analyst, or program manager). She suggests that the people, organizations, or industries that represent each of the boxes in her model all contain opportunities for you to check out—as learning and growth opportunities to consider or as career options in the future. I've put together some examples here to give you an idea of how you might adapt this model yourself—and I've included some possible people, organizations, or industries you might explore (using "public librarian" as an example).

### Suppliers Who Feed in Materials and Services

- book publishers
  - textbooks and e-textbooks
  - children, young adult, and adult book publishers and e-publishers
- distributors of digital content
- manufacturers of library displays, equipment, furniture, and supplies
- digitization, microfilming, cataloging, and related services
- automation, scanners, and RFID services and products

### The Work Engages with the Community or Other Outside Partners (Use in Place of "The Work Is Regulated," Which She Uses in Her Model)

- schools
- senior centers
- social service agencies

### The Work Is Managed

- library administration
- museum, gallery, and other special library workplaces' administration
- information organization administration, or some department within the organization

### The Work Feeds into Other Work

- consulting work
- associations and organizations related to particular subject areas represented in libraries (e.g., medicine, health care, health issues, business,

hobbies, travel and tourism, an array of social services, etc.) or in information organizations

- solopreneur: independent information professional

### *Professional Associations That Support the Work*

- national, regional, and state-level library or information services–related associations
- nonprofit educational and literacy-related associations and foundations

### *Experts Who Feed in Knowledge about How to Do the Work*

- university program administrators
- university-level faculty
- experts in various subjects who work with organizations that provide learning opportunities

If you take the time to consider ways to adapt this model, you'll find out more about different, yet complementary, types of work in different sectors. This information can help you decide if you want to invest more time and effort into learning about opportunities within these sectors (where your skills, knowledge, and experience will work to your benefit). Here are some ways you can do that:

- Conduct informational interviews with individuals you've come to know through their visits to your workplace to complete their own work—or with those you've met in the exhibit halls at conferences where they are vendors.
- Read more about the work they do and the products or services they provide through a visit to their website.
- Take a vocation vacation to do a "trial run" of the work you're interested in.
- Learn more about the occupations, themselves, through the Bureau of Labor's O*NET site.[16]
- Job shadow someone who is doing the particular work you're interested in.

In whatever way you decide to pursue this type of learning opportunity, adapted from Power's model, once you've done it, you should definitely know more about a potential area than you did before you took on this activity.

### If You Want to Go Deeper in a Particular Area You're Already Familiar with (or Deeper in Something That Interests You)

Step out of your comfort zone—beyond what you already know well.

- Speak and present.
- Take an advanced seminar.
- Pursue a certificate program.
- Write a paper or book about what you know and love—I promise the experience will take you even deeper into the area in which you're fascinated.

### If You're Trying to Reignite Some Passion Back into Your Work

Revisit why you joined your field in the first place. What excited you about LIS work? How did you hope to make a difference? Is the initial vision you had for yourself the same now? Or has it changed? What do you need to relight that passion again? Perhaps shifting your priorities in your work (with the help of your boss) so you can do more of what you love? Will it help to spend some vacation time at a place that lets you explore new ideas or new possibilities for yourself? There are many books, videos, and people who can help you get back in touch with what's most important to you—it's worth it to invest your time and effort in exploring this important area.

### If You're Interested in Advocacy

Advocacy work can take many forms. Consider these:

- Join groups within your association that focus on advocacy for issues that are most important to you. Become active.
- Investigate local nonprofits that could use your talents and skills, either as a volunteer or for part-time work.
- Speak.
- Write.
- Offer debriefs to your organization on the advocacy work you're doing and how it can make a difference inside your organization.

### If You Want to Prepare for Advancement and Career Moves into More Senior Positions

One of your first learning goals—if you are considering moving up into leadership or other more senior roles—is to find out what it takes to move up, either in your current location or in others. Many possibilities are available to you:

- informational interviewing
- shadowing
- mentorship from leaders you admire
- reading profiles or listening to podcasts from those who have moved into senior roles
- joining a community leadership initiative or a similar initiative within the library world like the Emerging Leaders Program sponsored by ALA
- certification (for example, the CPLA [Certified Public Library Administrator] or the Advanced Certificate in Strategic Management of Digital Assets and Services—there are many available, depending on your area of focus)

### If the Budget (Yours or Your Organization's) Is Tight

First, check to see just how much is in the budget for you to spend. Once you know the specifics here, you'll be in a better position to consider your choices. You could

- check for scholarships, stipends, and chances to work a certain number of hours in exchange for a registration fee to a conference;
- check for reduced rates if you (or your organization) is part of an association;
- identify workshops, webinars, or podcasts that may offer early-bird rates to events;
- inquire about the possibility of splitting the fee with your organization (you contribute a certain percentage and your organization contributes the rest); and
- review "The What" list for opportunities that are cost-free.

### If You're Unemployed

- Check for special reduced rates for any learning event or online learning opportunity.
- Do the same for associations you're interested in—many offer special, time-limited rates for professionals currently seeking employment.
- Volunteer.

### If You're Transitioning to Retirement (but Still Want to Be Active in the Field)

- Continue to network with colleagues.
- Stay active in associations.
- Join a committee/task force/new initiative where you can continue to contribute once you have retired.

- Choose an area of interest you haven't had time to pursue while working—turn this area into your own special project (whether it's learning about a new specialty or writing an article, paper, or book related to the part of your work you're most passionate about).
- Mentor others.

### If You Want to Gain More Visibility

- Participate in more learning opportunities outside your organization.
- Attend national (or international) conferences.
- Present frequently.
- Speak at industry-related events.
- Lead.

### If You Want to Enrich Your Life Overall

This is the place where you can get as creative as you'd like! Consider what would be different, challenging, and delightful to you. Perhaps you've had an interest in travel, or experiencing different cultures, or offering your talents in new ways and new places. You could

- learn a new language,
- participate in Habitat for Humanity or other organizations with similar goals,
- travel to another country for study or pleasure,
- join Road Scholar events (formerly Elderhostel),
- join the International Federation of Library Associations and Institutions (IFLA),
- or read through and put into practice some ideas suggested in chapter 9 under "Practice Amazing Self-Care."

## Notes

1. Dicionary.com, "Opportunity," www.dictionary.com/browse/opportunity?s=t/.
2. SkillsYouNeed.com, "What is Coaching?," www.skillsyouneed.com/learn/coaching.html.
3. Tamara Acevedo, "The Accidental Librarian," in *Making the Most of Your Library Career,* ed. Lois Stickell and Bridgette Sanders (Chicago: American Library Association, 2014), 23.
4. Cynthia Mediavilla, "Conducting a Yearlong Fellowship Program," in *Continuing Education for Librarians,* ed. Carol Smallwood, Kerol Harrod, and Vera Gubnitskaia (Jefferson, NC: McFarland, 2013), 80.
5. Halelly Azulay, *Employee Development on a Shoestring* (Alexandria, VA: ASTD Press, 2012), 93.
6. Mark Koba, "Returnships for Older Workers: Proceed with Caution," *CNBC,* October 15, 2013, www.cnbc.com/2013/10/14/returnships-for-older-workers-proceed-with-caution.html.
7. Katharine Hansen, "Job Shadowing: An Overview," *Experience,* www.experience.com/advice/job-search/networking/job-shadowing-an-overview/.

8.   Azulay, *Employee Development*, 97.

9.   Barbara Sher and Annie Gottlieb, *Teamworks!* (New York: Grand Central Publishing, 1991).

10.  Young Adult Library Services Association (YALSA), "Current YALSA Task Forces," www.ala.org/yalsa/workingwithyalsa/tf/.

11.  Ron Carucci, "Why Everyone Needs a Portfolio Career," *Forbes*, September 25, 2017, www.forbes.com/sites/roncarucci/2017/09/25/three-reasons-everyone-needs-a-portfolio-career/#59ec4b5e4d07/.

12.  Michael Oden, "Best of Both Worlds: The Advantages of a Dual-Library Internship" *American Libraries Magazine*, January/February 2017, 31.

13.  Asha Pandey, "5 Killer Examples: How to Use Microlearning-Based Training Effectively," eLearning Industry, April 11, 2016, https://elearningindustry.com/5-killer-examples-use-microlearning-based-training-effectively/.

14.  Azulay, *Employee Development*, 39.

15.  Sally J. Power, *The Mid-Career Success Guide* (Westport, CT: Praeger, 2006), 41.

16.  US Department of Labor, "O*NET OnLine," www.onetonline.org/.

# CHAPTER 8

· · · · · · · · ·

# Turn an Opportunity into a Reality

Now that you have an idea of the range of growth opportunities that are available, it's time to put this information to use. The best way to do this is to take the possibilities for growth that you just read about in chapter 7, the data you've gathered about yourself through your own self-assessment in chapters 4 and 6, data about current workplace realities discussed in chapter 2, and emerging trends from chapter 5 and use all these important pieces of information to create your plan for turning opportunities into realities and move yourself forward. Not to worry—we'll walk through this process together in this chapter, so you can use it now or adapt it to meet your own specific needs in the future. There are two parts to turning opportunities into realities: (1) choosing specific opportunities and (2) translating them into actions you can pursue, beginning right now. It's a process you can repeat over and over again (or adapt) when you're ready to consider pursuing additional growth opportunities. Let's look at both parts so you can get going!

## Part 1: Get Clear on Your Best Bets

I hope that you're feeling energized and excited about starting this process. Though you may also be thinking, *Yes, I'm ready to go, but what's the best way to proceed from here?* You've got to start somewhere, and while there may be a dozen opportunities that look good to you, remember that you want your efforts to succeed; so let's make sure you choose a do-able path that sets you up for success along the way and builds momentum. For the rest of this chapter, I'll be referring to this path as your *Going for It!* Growth Plan, or simply, your Growth Plan.

By now, you should be able to describe, in detail, one or two particular ways you'd like to begin growing from wherever you are right now. Sure, you may already have identified a number of possibilities as you read through chapter 7. But for the purpose of this next activity (and to ensure you success as you launch your *Going for It!* Growth Plan), pick one or two ways you'd like to grow to get you started, keeping in mind the direction you think you'd like to explore first. Put that information in the space below by filling in the sentence stems you'll see there.

## Notes to Myself

This is how I'd like to grow starting right now!

- If I could dig deeper into an area I am most curious or most passionate about, it would be

  _____

- If I could broaden my skill set, the top two areas I would choose to gain new skills in would be

  _____

  _____

- Beyond the sector of librarianship or information services I know the most about, two other areas I would like explore include

  _____

  _____

- If I could choose one area I would like to be the go-to person in, it would be

  _____

  _____

- If I had my preferences about the manner in which I could begin growing from here, I would like to do so by pursuing them either: independently, as part of a group, within my work setting, outside my work setting, or through a combination of methods

_____

_____

- The top two growth opportunities that could most energize (or reenergize) me right now would be

_____

_____

Congratulations! You now have some specific ideas about opportunities that would most motivate you. Let's keep moving forward!

## Selecting Your Top Choices

It's time to start choosing. Let's start with your "wish list" (not to be confused with a to-do list). This wish list should be your first pass at identifying at least eight to ten opportunities that most appealed to you—or caught your attention—as you read through chapter 7.

 **Notes to Myself**

**In the spaces on the next page, fill in your top eight to ten choices of opportunities.** Feel free to also include opportunities that you're interested in that didn't get mentioned in the last chapter. At this point, don't worry about whether they are the best opportunities for you to pursue—we'll look at a number of ways you can test these choices throughout this chapter. For now, just fill in initial choices in this section. Also fill in a few words describing the appeal of each of your choices: What interests you about each one you have listed? How do you think each one could help you move your career forward? (Again, don't worry about the feasibility or the "appropriateness" of your choices right now.). And if you're not yet sure about your direction, that's fine too. Just note what you hope each growth opportunity you've listed will do for you, in terms of shedding light on things you are curious about or want to learn more about.

_____

_____

_____

_____

_____

_____

_____

_____

_____

We'll return to this list at the end of part 1. Just be sure to complete the list (above) before you go further so that you can refer to it as you read the rest of this section and complete the follow-up activity at the end of part 1.

## Time to Get Strategic

To choose the opportunities you'll be taking first to launch your Growth Plan, you'll want to make thoughtful decisions. The following suggestions will help you do just that—they will point out possible pitfalls you'll want to avoid and offer ideas for the most effective ideas that you'll want to consider as you put together your Growth Plan.

## Random Choices Won't Do It

A nice, numbered list of opportunities that you're most interested in is one way to start designing your Growth Plan—but it's not necessarily the most effective way, not if you really want to enjoy your pursuit of chosen growth opportunities as well as learn from them, build on them, and get the most out of them. A random list runs the risk of becoming just another one of those to-do lists—no different from any other list you make and don't always accomplish. Don't relegate your opportunities list to just another piece of paper that makes you sigh and feel guilty or overwhelmed at the end of your workday.

The Growth Plan you are creating is different. It represents a powerful tool for growing your career. Don't make it easy to dismiss or put off—it's your professional life and your future you're building here!

## Don't Run Around in Circles

Spending your time engaging in random activities can lead you to feel like you're running around in circles. The result can be demotivating and exhausting and leave you feeling like you don't have a sense of direction. You know that's *not* the case—not if you've taken the time to really work through this book and reflect on what you've learned. If you have done those things, then it's quite likely you *do* have a sense of direction—perhaps it's moving closer to shaping a professional life and career that gives you more satisfaction and a sense of challenge. Or maybe it's building on the passion that is already a part of your professional life right now. Whatever your direction is (even if it is a tentative one), let's get you moving toward it right now, with the help of some strategizing.

## Put Strategy to Work for You

Consider strategy your personal compass for going forward and an essential element of your Growth Plan. Strategizing your own *Going for It!* Growth Plan can take into account a number of different variables, depending on the direction *you* want to be heading and *your* personal circumstances. A broad strategic Growth Plan will likely take into account the parameters that you'll see in the next section. As you read through them, consider them to be guidelines for testing the soundness of each opportunity you are considering.

- *Movement in the right direction.* Will pursuing a particular growth opportunity bring you closer to your own goal(s) of increased satisfaction or engagement? Will it move you toward a longer-term goal of moving into a leadership role, giving you greater depth of knowledge in your chosen area or broader skills across a wider range of librarianship or information services? Will it give you the chance to explore alternatives outside traditional library roles—or any other goal(s) you have identified for yourself?

- *A mix of both shorter-term and longer-term growth opportunities.* Let's say you want to grow your leadership skills. Some shorter-term opportunities you could pursue that would let you do that could include reading books and articles related to leadership or observing and then reflecting on a leader you admire when you see him in action. A longer-term growth opportunity might include joining the Emerging Leaders Program that is part of ALA.[1] Or it could mean volunteering to lead a task force for an issue you feel strongly about.

- *A consideration of the time involved* in taking on a particular growth opportunity. Will it be do-able, given the other demands on your time—or if it's not, can you make it do-able?

- *A consideration of the costs involved.* Is the particular growth opportunity you're considering free? Will it cost money to pursue? If so, how will it be funded?

- *Your level of excitement/interest* for pursuing this opportunity. Will you look forward to engaging in it?

- *Usability.* Will you be able to demonstrate or implement your new learning on your job right now? If that isn't possible, how will you keep your new learning "fresh" until you can put it to use?

- *Support.* Will you have support for pursuing this opportunity? That includes support from your supervisor, mentor, colleagues, or friends and family members (or all of them!). If your answer is yes, that's great! Is the support contingent on your doing something in return for the support? If you will need to do something in return (make a presentation or take on new responsibilities afterward, for example), will this type of reciprocating be feasible given other responsibilities you have right now? Can you negotiate with your supervisor on ways you could reciprocate or give back to your organization? If your answer is, "No, I won't have support from others at all," how will you keep yourself motivated throughout your pursuit of this opportunity?

# The Power of Career Conversations

Career conversations offer a great way to discuss, get feedback on, and ask about ways you can pursue growth opportunities. They have become quite a popular trend inside organizations today. Career conversations are used as a recruitment tool, retention tool, engagement tool, and overall go-to solution for employee development. This is good news, as it highlights the value of conducting employer-employee (or manager-worker) ongoing discussions. Such conversations offer workers fantastic resources and support from their employers and can be a boon to employees' growth and commitment to their organizations. So learning more about them and utilizing them are well worth your time as a way to continue growing your career inside the organization you work for (if that is one of the options you wish to pursue).

However, there are some challenges that can make these conversations more difficult. One challenge is that an organization may agree that holding career conversations with employees is a great idea; but simply *saying that* is not enough. Managers who conduct career conversations with those who report to them need to have the training and interest to hold these discussions. Many managers are very busy themselves and may see these discussions as another responsibility that eats up their time. Or they may confuse career conversations with performance reviews, which they are *not*. Others may not feel comfortable conducting such conversations. Though these issues could lead to some derailed conversations, for the most part, managers and supervisors see such discussions as positive and powerful ways to nurture their employees' careers and commitment—and so they're happy to do them! One interesting point here: much of the discussions, articles, webinars, and books about career conversations are from the employer's perspective—helping those in management better understand and conduct career conversations. There isn't a lot available to help you, the employee, either initiate or best maximize these discussions.

So let's start there—with the perspective from your side of the fence. How can you get the most from career conversations? First, let's look at just what career conversations are meant to be. Productive and meaningful career conversations are simply ongoing discussions with your boss about your career development and growth in the organization. They can be brief (as short as ten minutes), but they need to happen regularly (whatever the two of you decide will work best schedule-wise). Career conversations are not performance reviews or yearly evaluations. The purpose of career discussions is simply to focus on how you can continue growing, contributing to the organization's bottom line, and asking for and receiving constructive feedback on how you might improve or grow your skill set as well as what the next step forward for you might be. Not all these items need to be covered in one meeting, but these topics are ones that generally come up during career conversations.

Your organization may already use career conversations as a tool to help you develop your career. And your boss may already be well-versed in how to conduct these conversations. If so, that's great! Just make sure that you're taking full advantage of them and do your part to contribute meaningful questions—and answers—to these conversations.

If your organization doesn't already have a practice of having managers hold career conversations with the people who report to them, or if your manager is charged with doing so but seems to run these discussions reluctantly, then it's likely you'll need to step up to either initiate career conversations or help your manager turn the meetings into productive and positive ones.

Let's look at initiating first. Though this section suggests some ideas for how to initiate a career conversation, there are no specific templates or words you need to use. Instead, consider what you're asking for (especially as it relates to pursuing your chosen growth opportunities), why you're asking for it, and, in your own words, how you can request regular career conversations in ways that benefit you and your boss. Consider the relationship you've already built with your boss. Have you worked together for a while? Or is this a manager whom you've only known for a brief time period? Is this person aware of your career aspirations, your areas of expertise, your strengths, and areas you're most passionate about? If your boss already knows quite a bit about you, then simply asking for the time to sit down with this person to talk more about your future growth and ways you'd like to contribute or up your skill set might be just right. Then at that meeting, you can let your boss know your interest in turning this initial conversation into regular, brief meetings. If your boss and you do not yet know one another well, then your request for a career conversation may need to be more formal—though the message remains the same—you would like to meet to talk about your career future and some ideas you have for how you would like to contribute. Asking for a specific time and suggesting a certain length for your meeting can help your boss plan for it a bit better.

To prepare for your meeting, do your homework. Note what you'll want your boss to know about how you think that you, your boss, and your organization could benefit from these meetings. Put together a list of your more recent work projects, committees, or task forces you've been a part of; your recent accomplishments; and anything else you think would help your boss get up to speed with your current profile. Also put together a list of things you would like to discuss during these meetings (in collaboration with what your boss believes would be useful to discuss). This might include constructive feedback on your performance, an assessment of your skills, a conversation about your career goals, or a conversation about growth opportunities within your organization (to name just a few).

Now for the growth opportunities part: Your boss can be a valuable resource for you in supporting, endorsing, approving of, and generally helping you identify and pursue growth opportunities. During these conversations, if you are able to share with your boss the particular ways you'd like to grow and how you think these growth opportunities would improve your performance or your ability to contribute to your organization or better support your team's goals, then you stand a good chance of being supported in your efforts.

If, on the other hand, you want to pursue growth opportunities on your own, outside your workplace—or if the opportunities you want to pursue don't have a direct bearing on your current work—then you probably don't need to go into detail or even ask for approval. Still, holding ongoing career conversations with your boss is a good idea. It gives your boss a "heads-up" about your interest in growing, and in the future, these conversations may lead to other opportunities.

After the first or any subsequent career conversation, keep a few notes of what was discussed as well as any follow-up that needs to be done. It doesn't hurt to send a note to your boss summarizing your meeting, extending appreciation for the time (if you feel that is appropriate), and confirming the date of the next meeting.

Career conversations don't have to be held exclusively with your boss. Having these types of discussions with a mentor you're working with is also a great idea. There may be times when your boss is stretched too thin to be able to agree to regular meetings with you. If that is the case, then it is all the more important to have others you can establish a regular pattern of career conversations with.

## What's in It for Your Employer?

It is in the best interests of employers to encourage professional development and growth opportunities. Though ongoing development remains ultimately your responsibility (and that's a good thing), your growth and development benefit your organization as well (also a good thing!). A recent blog post, "How to Help Build Employees' Career Paths So They Don't Quit," described a survey done by American Psychological Association's Center for Organizational Excellence.[2] The survey found that a high percentage of US workers who were worried about how their jobs were changing and were not getting career development support from their bosses tended to not be motivated to do their best work—and, to make matters worse, they tended to leave![3]

## What's Learning Got to Do with It?

To answer this question posed above: Learning has *everything* to do with turning opportunities into realities. Think about it: you've already invested a considerable amount of time, energy, and reflection in your decision to pursue growth opportunities. You've assessed yourself, thought about how you want to make a difference, considered what you want to bring to the table, and reflected on how growth opportunities will make your career more meaningful.

Now is the time to make sure you get the most from any growth opportunity you choose to pursue. It would be silly—downright foolish—to choose an opportunity and then go after it half-heartedly or with little idea as to how you can maximize the opportunity. You want to pursue any chance to grow with a 100 percent commitment to finishing whatever you start and feeling good about the results.

Taking on just about any growth opportunity will quite likely involve *new learning*—stretching yourself to pick up new knowledge, a new skill set, or any number of new ways of going about your work. Because you're investing your (limited) time and energy in this learning, it's worthwhile to take a closer look at learning itself, especially as it relates to pursuing growth opportunities so you can make the most of your efforts.

For instance, consider how you might answer questions like these before choosing a particular growth opportunity and launching your new endeavor:

## How Do You Learn Best?

Do you enjoy learning alone? With others? Through self-discovery? Through guidance and the expertise of others? Perhaps a combination of all these ways? Pursuing growth opportunities shouldn't feel like a never-ending homework assignment. Nor should it feel like it focuses on all the ways you don't like to learn. For example, some individuals love online learning. Others prefer to be surrounded by fellow learners who are all discovering something new together. Take the time to think about how *you* learn best and choose opportunities where you can leverage your preferred way of learning.

## What Makes Learning Exciting to You?

Rather than feeling boring, scary, or overwhelming, what makes learning exciting to you? Remember that growth opportunities are meant to be interesting, fun, and pleasurable experiences. Sure, learning something new may be a bit scary at times for all of us—but, for the most part, the experience should be one you enjoy.

## Do You Know What You Don't Know?

Given the growing breadth of the LIS field and the increasing expectations of those who turn to library and information professionals for answers, the learning curve for LIS workers has never been steeper. Because of this, it can be useful to regularly assess your own levels of understanding of new technologies, services, and the latest and best practices, especially in your particular specialty area. The good news is that once you've identified a gap in your knowledge or skill set (and we all have these gaps, no matter what our field—the world moves too quickly for it to be otherwise), then you have a better idea where you want to put your time and efforts. You know what you need to work on—which means you know how to add more value, and you are free to choose the way in which you want to do that.

## Do You Know How to Leverage OTJ (On the Job) Learning?

Liane Davey, writing for *Harvard Business Review*, offers some great ideas for taking your desire to learn and grow and placing that desire right in the middle of your workday, where you can leverage a particular growth opportunity you wish to pursue.[4] For instance, as a library staffer, let's say you want to learn more about—or become more skilled in—customer service. Following Davey's suggestions, first, investigate all you can about customer service by going online—look for free resources, YouTube videos, podcasts, and so on related to customer service. What you'll probably notice is that customer service has many, many components, including listening skills, maintaining a calm demeanor, asking the right questions, and checking for understanding (to name just a few). As you determine which components you want to learn more about, hone in on them by reading more targeted articles, finding and reviewing case studies on customer service across a variety of settings, and observing colleagues and friends who seem to really do a great job at it. Then experiment yourself by trying out some of what you've learned with those you serve (students, patrons, committee members, community partners) to see how well you're doing. Practice, ask for feedback from a trusted coworker, log your efforts, and note what you're doing well and what you still want to work on. Before you know it, you'll find that what began as a learning assignment you've given yourself has turned into a new or highly improved skill set, and you'll have the satisfying feeling of knowing you've turned a growth opportunity into a reality.

## The Value of Chunking

Take the advice of Allyce Barron, a training specialist. She recommends chunking, or breaking learning into smaller, more manageable pieces. When it comes to your learning objectives, she suggests, "Choose only one. You've pared down the number of resources coming at you, but now when you read a journal, watch a webinar, or attend a conference, the question becomes, 'What is the one skill or piece of knowledge that I am going to apply to the current project I identified earlier?' The answer must be relevant and easily implementable."[5]

# The Practicalities of Making Opportunities Happen

To increase the likelihood of your choices becoming realities, you will want to consider some practical questions before you launch your Growth Plan. Here are some of those key questions.

## Is Funding Available?

Depending on the opportunity you wish to pursue, there may be a cost attached to it. While some pursuits like shadowing, networking with colleagues in the same geographical area, joining a local committee, or attending continuing education events sponsored by your employer (and other similar options) may be cost-free, other options may not be. Don't let that stop you in your tracks. Instead, investigate. Find out about alternatives to needing to pay in full. Look into these ideas.

## Is Time Available?

Often, pursuing your growth opportunities will require that you engage in them during your workday. Since you can't simply walk away from you daily responsibilities to go after a growth opportunity, you'll often need the approval of someone else. Or you'll need to come up with a plan to give you the block of time you'll need. Assuming you will need to check in with someone to ask about freeing up some of your time, see if one of these ideas might work:

- Can you adjust your work schedule (temporarily) to have the time available when you need it?
- Can you detail a plan to present to your supervisor that shows the benefit of having time for a particular activity?
- Can you offer to present to other staff members (or write an article) on the topic you're going to learn about during your release time?

Even if you have the option of pursuing a particular growth opportunity during your off-time, you'll still want to consider the time it will take.

## Time to Look Back at Your Top Choices

Now that you've had the chance to view your potential growth opportunities from a number of perspectives, let's put them to the test to see which ones might be the best ones for you to begin your journey of intentional, strategic growth. Use the "Meets My Criteria Checklist" in the next section to see how each opportunity fits for you right now. Here are suggestions for completing the checklist and for making it a useful tool for you.

1. With the checklist on pages 156 and 157, copy the top ten growth opportunities that you listed earlier in this chapter down the left-hand column (fill this same list of opportunities in the left-hand column on page 2 of the checklist).

2. Next, look at the headings of each of the columns to the right of the "Growth Opportunities" column.

3. For each opportunity you listed, respond to the question posed at the top of each column by putting a check mark in the appropriate box or leaving it blank, depending on how you answer the question posed in the column heading. For instance, let's say that the first growth opportunity you've written in is "attend one-hour webinar on how libraries can prepare high school students for the future." After you've written that in, you would then look to the next column, titled "Short term," and you would put a check in that box because attending a one-hour webinar is a short-term activity. If this was a six-month opportunity you listed, you would put a check in the box under the column titled "Long term."

4. Then look to the next columns, working your way from left to right, and put check marks in the boxes that fit for that growth opportunity. For example, if the topic of that one-hour webinar is "Personally meaningful," put a check mark in the corresponding box. If the one-hour webinar is "Positively challenging," put a check mark in the box that corresponds with that column heading for that opportunity. But if it's not "Professionally on-target," you wouldn't put a check mark in that box.

5. For the column titled "What are the costs?" fill in the word *free* or put in the amount (in dollars) that this opportunity will cost you.

6. When you have completed page one, look at the second page to continue filling out your checklist. Be sure you have copied all the growth opportunities that you listed on the first page onto page 2 of the checklist. Then you are ready to repeat the process of filling in a check mark for those items that meet the criteria listed at the top of each column.

| Growth opportunities | Short term | Long term | Interests me? | Personally meaningful? | Positively challenging? | Professionally on-target? | What are the costs? | Is time available? |
|---|---|---|---|---|---|---|---|---|
|  |  |  |  |  |  |  |  |  |
|  |  |  |  |  |  |  |  |  |
|  |  |  |  |  |  |  |  |  |
|  |  |  |  |  |  |  |  |  |
|  |  |  |  |  |  |  |  |  |
|  |  |  |  |  |  |  |  |  |
|  |  |  |  |  |  |  |  |  |
|  |  |  |  |  |  |  |  |  |

**Figure 8.1.** Meets my criteria checklist

| Growth opportunities | What do I hope to learn? | Reflects my values? | Risk level OK? | Does it take me in direction I want to go? | Other criteria important to me? |
|---|---|---|---|---|---|
|  |  |  |  |  |  |
|  |  |  |  |  |  |
|  |  |  |  |  |  |
|  |  |  |  |  |  |
|  |  |  |  |  |  |
|  |  |  |  |  |  |
|  |  |  |  |  |  |
|  |  |  |  |  |  |
|  |  |  |  |  |  |
|  |  |  |  |  |  |

**Figure 8.1.** Meets my criteria checklist (cont.)

7. For the column titled "What do I hope to learn?" write in a short phrase that answers that question.

8. For the column titled "Other criteria important to me?" write in any phrase that represents something else you want to consider in helping you determine if this is a good opportunity for you.

9. When you're finished, look over your checklist and make sure you've filled in a response for each of your opportunities and for each of the headings on page 1 and page 2 of the checklist.

10. Look at your list of opportunities once you've listed them all and placed checkmarks in (or left blank) the appropriate boxes and written in any other comments in other boxes.

This completed checklist should help you narrow down your two to four top choices as the places to begin your pursuit of the best opportunities.

## Summary of Steps for Beginning to Choose Opportunities

1. To start, list eight to ten growth opportunities that most attract you.

2. Reflect on the direction you think you may want to be heading, in terms of growing your career, at this time.

3. Use the "Meets My Criteria Checklist" to evaluate and rank your list of chosen opportunities. After you have filled out the checklist, place a #1 next to your first choice, #2 next to your second choice, and then rank all your other choices.

4. Schedule a career conversation with your boss, mentor, trusted colleague, or friend (someone you've already shared your Growth Plan with) *if you feel a conversation with this person would be helpful.* Share your short list of possible opportunities that you're thinking of pursuing. Explain your rationale for choosing them and how they fit into your overall Growth Plan. Ask for feedback and any ideas or suggestions he or she may have that could help you at this time. Be specific—talking in generalities doesn't give you the clarity you're looking for right now. If you're sharing this information with your boss or supervisor, let him or her know that at this time, you're just asking for feedback. You're not ready to formally commit to beginning your pursuit of these opportunities yet. You will be doing that after you

have finished this chapter and chapter 9 and after you've filled in the first two sections of your Growth Plan in the final section of this book.

5.  Reflect on the feedback from others and amend your choices as you see fit.

6.  Submit any forms, paperwork, or applications needed to participate in your chosen growth opportunities (class enrollment form, webinar or conference registration, requests for time off—anything that needs to get done to actually start your new growth opportunity).

7.  Consider when you want to begin pursuing these opportunities and, if appropriate, think about a timeline for completing each of these activities. Or, if the opportunities you are pursuing are longer-term activities/actions on your part, think about and note different milestone markers in a calendar to gauge your progress on the way to fulfilling a particular activity/action that this growth opportunity represents. (You will do this more formally as you begin to create your Growth Plan through an activity at the end of this chapter.)

## Part 2: From Great Ideas to Going for It

OK, so you're officially "ready to launch"! Excellent! Your official start may be something as simple as showing up for a staff training or shadowing a leader you admire. Or it may be as complex as traveling out of state or even out of the country to attend or present at a large conference. It may mean altering your daily or weekly schedule to accommodate an evening class or volunteering at an organization over your weekends. No matter what it is, you're entering new territory. So you may feel both excited and a bit anxious. That's only natural.

### Caution: Possible Bumps Ahead!

Bumps can show up in all shapes and sizes. Some may look like permanent roadblocks that seem impossible to get over, or they can appear as detours (easy ones or more challenging ones) that require a shift in direction. Let's look closer at them so they don't blindside you when they present themselves.

Here are some ways you can recognize them:

- When what you're pursuing just isn't feeling right and your actions seem more like drudgery than delight. (Hint: You find yourself wondering, *Do I have to keep doing this?*)

- When you're gaining new knowledge or skills, but the more you learn, the more you realize the area you're pursuing just doesn't appeal to you. (This happened to me when I took an advanced photography class and realized that all the technical steps involved just didn't fit my nontechie temperament.)

- When the opportunity you chose keeps you feeling overwhelmed (or underwhelmed).

- When committing 100 percent to this opportunity is taking far more time or effort than you expected.

- When the opportunity is just not a good fit for you.

- When the direction the opportunity is taking you seems to be moving you further away from your growth goals—not closer to them.

There may be others that seem to be showstoppers for you—or at the least, they may cause you to pause, unsure how to go forward from where you are. Probably the most important thing to remember if unexpected bumps catch you by surprise is this: growth always has some element of risk to it. Each time we step out of our comfort zone, we step into an unknown adventure (I realize that although this may sound somewhat comforting, you probably want some practical ideas for dealing with your situation too!). So read on.

The second most important thing to realize when you hit a bump is that you have several options open to you. Think of your obstacle as a temporary one and consider what actions you can take. For example, if you're over- (or under-) whelmed, think about whether you could ratchet the experience up or down to make it fit better for you.

Let's say you're shadowing a colleague who creates and delivers outreach programs for at-risk youth. You are doing this because you have an interest in learning more about outreach initiatives—and you think that one day you'd like to do outreach programming yourself, eventually becoming a director of outreach programming. However, the shadowing you've been doing feels too passive, and it's getting a bit boring. Could you talk to your colleague about the possibility of codesigning a program? How about partnering with her on the delivery of a program?

Or what if you experience the opposite dilemma? What if that accelerated course you're taking is a bit too . . . accelerated? Can you opt to retake the course when it's offered at "regular" speed? Sure, it may take longer, but if it's an area you're truly interested in, wouldn't it be better to set yourself up for success in the longer term?

If the time or effort involved in pursuing a growth opportunity turns out to not be feasible, given your work schedule or lifestyle, can you try "chunking" (discussed earlier in this chapter)? Can you break this opportunity into smaller pieces and work on one piece at a time?

If you're in the midst of pursuing a growth opportunity and you realize "This just isn't for me; it doesn't fit who I am or what I want to be doing"—sort of what I experienced taking golf lessons—why not acknowledge that fact? And do so without guilting yourself too! Think of it this way: you've just discovered one particular activity that doesn't fit for you—out of dozens that may fit very well.

Take author Seth Godin's advice here: when it comes to deciding to quit, do so strategically. Not when you're feeling the angst, frustration, or disappointment in the midst of pursuing your opportunity and your obstacle pops up—but before you ever get started. Sounds a bit confusing, doesn't it? Let me explain: Godin's wisdom here is about determining ahead of time—before your pursuit of an opportunity begins—the circumstances under which you'll quit if things aren't going in the direction you had hoped for. This doesn't mean simply quitting when things get tough, or complicated, or when you're pushing yourself to take a new action or apply a difficult (at least difficult-at-first) concept. In other words, don't quit just because the pursuit is a bit harder than you thought it would be. Godin puts it this way: "Write down under what circumstances you're willing to quit. And when. And then stick with it."[6] He goes on to say, "If quitting is going to be a strategic decision that enables you to make smart choices . . . then you should outline your quitting strategy before the discomfort sets in." Quitting for the right reasons (right for you) frees up your energy and time so that you can pursue other growth opportunities more in line with what works for you and sends you in the right direction. Once you've made the decision to end the pursuit of a particular growth opportunity for all the right reasons, be certain that you follow this up with moving on to another opportunity that can reenergize you again and get you back on track.

My guess is that you can come up with alternatives or ways around your roadblock (or even quit strategically) if you take the time to reflect—rather than simply throw your hands up in frustration. Often, a trusted friend or colleague can help you brainstorm your options—and help you see possibilities you didn't see yourself.

One final point to keep in mind to get you past these moments of frustration: before you move on from that nasty bump you encountered, take the time to reflect on what you learned from this experience. Sure, you may have learned perseverance—but I bet you learned other things about yourself as well. You may know more about what you do and don't like. You may have a greater appreciation of the strengths and skill sets you really want to use. And you may have a better idea of the types of opportunities that truly say yes to you, as well as the ones that say "no, this one isn't for me."

## Get the Most from Your Growth Opportunities

Your Growth Plan and the pursuit of your chosen opportunities are important ways to grow yourself and your career. So you'll want to make sure you're getting the most that you can from each activity you participate in. Here are some ideas to do just that:

- Take the time to reflect on what you're learning from each opportunity you pursue. There are three points in time you need to build in. *Before* you begin, write down some goals for engaging in this activity. *During* the activity, keep a record of what you're learning, how this applies to the ways you want to grow your career, and anything else that you're finding or learning that are unexpected. *After* you complete the activity, reflect on what you learned—both the knowledge or skills gained—as well as what you learned about yourself. Take notes on how you hope to apply what you've learned and how your learning can be a catalyst for other activities you may decide to pursue in the future.

- Share your learning with others at staff meetings, networking groups, or anywhere you're comfortable with sharing.

- Think *application* all the time. Ask yourself, *How can I apply what I've just learned?*

- Keep track of all your growth opportunity "experiments." They will come in handy for networking purposes, résumés, online profiles, applications for grants or scholarships, and a dozen other ways. If you're like most professionals I know, you promise yourself you will write down all the development activities you've participated in and everything you've learned but then you get sidetracked by other responsibilities. Time passes and you find it a bit challenging to remember the substance of webinars you attended (even those you loved), or the person you met at a networking event, or the great customer service model you learned about in a class that you would love to adapt for the group you serve. So keep track of these growth opportunities regularly. Find a system that works for you and make it a regular part of your professional growth.

Last, consider applying the advice that Diane Belcher, senior director at Harvard Business Publishing, uses with her own team after a meeting. She asks those on her team what they've just learned, how it can be applied to their roles, or how their new knowledge can help better serve clients.[7] You can do the very same thing—ask yourself these application-focused questions and you're more likely to put your new learning to work much more quickly.

## Time to Begin Formulating Your Growth Plan!

You have worked really hard to get to this point. Congratulations! It's time to start building your Growth Plan using the information you've gathered in all the chapters you have read so far. Here is how you can begin:

1. Review the notes you wrote down earlier in this chapter under the "This is how I'd like to grow starting right now" section and under the list of your eight to ten top opportunity choices you would like to pursue.
2. After reviewing your notes, turn to the final section of this book: "My *Going for It!* Growth Plan."
3. Under section 1 in the Growth Plan, fill in a summary of your thoughts on how you would like to begin growing right now (based on your notes from chapter 8 that I've just suggested you review).
4. Under section 2 in the Growth Plan, list between two and four opportunities (taken from your notes in chapter 8, which I have suggested you review) that you want to start pursuing first. Include a mix of both short-term and longer-term opportunities.
5. Also under section 2, list your timeline for when you are going to begin to pursue each opportunity that you have listed there and your anticipated dates for completing both the shorter-term and longer-term opportunities.

Great! You've started to build your Growth Plan! That's as far as you need to go for now. You will fill in the remaining sections of your Growth Plan after you have finished reading chapter 9.

There is one last section in this chapter that you will want to look over. It offers suggestions for implementing your chosen opportunities. And it builds on information you just filled in for the start of your Growth Plan in the final section of this book. You can use the process you'll read on the next page over and over again as you get ready to pursue new growth opportunities.

## How to Begin Implementing Your Chosen Opportunities

1. Review what you have listed in section 2 of your Growth Plan. Doing so will remind you of where you want to start.

2. Look at the first opportunity you have listed in your long-term opportunities list.

3. Determine if this is an opportunity that you can begin on your own or if it is one that you need to get approval for first before you can go any further.

4. Also determine if it is one that has its own timeline for registering for it or for showing up for (for example: an online class, traditional class, webinar, podcast, or associate-related activity/committee usually has its own start date).

5. Complete whatever forms you need in order to sign up for, register for, let someone know of your intent to participate in, and so on.

6. If this opportunity is one that you need to keep track of for someone else (like your boss), make sure you know exactly what is required for you to do so.

7. Get any needed materials (texts, etc.) beforehand.

8. Find out if there are other things you need to do before starting, such as filling in a survey or submitting your profile online (many e-courses may ask you to "introduce yourself" in some way to your fellow participants).

9. If this is something you are doing independently, make sure you've identified a quiet place (whether at home, in the office, in your library, etc.) to be able to fully participate without interruption.

10. If this is an opportunity in which you will have fellow participants, get to know them. It will give you a chance to learn more about them, and they may turn out to be colleagues or valuable individuals in your network in the future.

11. Document the completion of your opportunity in some way—perhaps on your calendar, your online profile, or your file of "courses completed." The final section of this book will offer suggestions for reflecting on each opportunity after you've completed it.

12. Go through this same process for each opportunity you intend to pursue.

# Notes

1.  American Library Association, "ALA Emerging Leaders Program," www.ala.org/educationcareers/leadership/emergingleaders/.
2.  Gwen Moran, "How to Help Build Employees' Career Paths So They Don't Quit," *American Psychological Association's Center for Organizational Excellence*, November 3, 2017, www.fastcompany.com/40490723/how-to-help-build-employees-career-paths-so-they-dont-quit/.
3.  Ibid.
4.  Liane Davey, "You Can Learn and Get Work Done at the Same Time," *Harvard Business Review*, January 11, 2016, https://hbr.org/2016/01/you-can-learn-and-get-work-done-at-the-same-time/.
5.  Allyce Barron, "Professional Development, One Bite at a Time," *Training & Development*, March 2014, 70–73.
6.  Seth Godin, *The Dip: A Little Book That Teaches You When to Quit (and When to Stick)* (New York: Penguin Group, 2007), 71.
7.  Moran, "How to Help Build."

# CHAPTER 9

· · · · · · · · · ·

## Icing on Your Cake

This chapter is about doubling—or even tripling—the value you can derive from following the suggestions, tools, and practices you've learned about in this book. Assuming you have accepted the invitation that this book offered in its introduction—to say yes to exploring new possibilities—you've taken the time to thoughtfully reflect on the questions this book raises, and you've filled in the "Notes to Myself" activities, you have the makings of a solid Growth Plan for yourself already. But hang on, as this chapter, "Icing on Your Cake," can make an even bigger difference in your efforts going forward.

The focus of this chapter is offering you tools to set yourself up for success. How? It offers ideas you can use to enhance the other actions you have read about in previous chapters. It suggests ways to put your best self into your efforts, and it helps you rekindle a sense of joy in whatever it is that you're doing. Read on and gather even more tools for growing and thriving in your career.

## Make the Most of Every Interaction

At this point, you're well on your way to recognizing opportunities to grow your career—and you've probably already begun planning how to take advantage of some specific ones. Perhaps you've already started pursuing opportunities that you're most excited about. That's great! I encourage you to stretch your thinking even a bit more. In the same way that we grow accustomed to our lives' daily routines, we also grow accustomed to the daily or weekly work interactions that we engage in regularly. These interactions with others can become so routine that we almost do them on autopilot at times. However, I suggest that you don't take these interactions for granted. Instead, consider them to be bonuses—extra chances to extend yourself and grow your career simply by taking the time to thoughtfully engage with whomever you encounter.

Have a look at some activities that you probably engage in regularly: coffee breaks; lunches with colleagues; staff meetings; committee meetings; quarterly, semiannual, or annual meetings with larger groups from your organization; retreats that feature guest speakers from inside or outside your field; regional meetings; association meetings in your city, state, region, or at the national level; as well as meetings with "sister" associations that focus on work that complements your own. Every one of these instances of interacting with others can be an even richer experience. How? By thoughtfully engaging with others *every time*—for example: learning more about a project that a coworker is involved in, finding out about a cool new technology a colleague is trying out in her library, or finding out how a presentation went for a coworker when he spoke at a recent conference. In our overly scheduled, technology-enhanced, and way-too-busy workdays, brief but meaningful interactions with others gives you a chance to pause, connect, and reenergize yourself. They also let you talk about your career in authentic, rather than superficial, ways.

These meetings, get-togethers, and events offer opportunities to talk with colleagues, managers, leaders, big thinkers in the field, and thought-provoking individuals whose words inspire you or get you thinking about new possibilities. Here are some ideas you may want to try to deepen your interactions with others—as well as get ideas for growing your career the next time you have the opportunity to share a few moments with someone while you're engaged in some professional activity.

At presentations,

- Take the time after a meeting or presentation to introduce yourself to at least two or three people. Or introduce yourself to the speaker(s).
- Tell the speakers what you liked about their presentation.
- Ask a question about how their research or project might apply to your own area of expertise or the people you serve.
- Let them know you appreciate their particular approach—and give an example of what aspect of their work you're referring to.
- Ask more about the things they think will be important in your field over the next five years.

While interacting with colleagues,

- Ask a few colleagues if they've been to any interesting presentations or conferences lately—and what they learned from them—or offer to share what you learned at an event you attended.

- Find out what a coworker is doing in her job that's different since the last time the two of you talked.
- Ask a colleague from a different work setting what new technologies (or programs or services) he's trying out in his setting.
- Ask anyone you have a conversation with about the latest thing they read or listened to that impressed them.

As you engage with others and learn from them, consider how the substance of your conversation with them might help you in strategizing your own future career growth.

These same ideas for reaching out to others can be adapted to the webinars, podcasts, or video presentations you watch or listen to on your laptop. Right now, think about the ones you listened to or watched over the last four months or so. Reflect on the ones that were most informative and interesting to you. Dig out the notes you took at the time to more clearly recall the presentation. List these presentations in the spaces below, along with what you most appreciated about each one—or what you learned, or how you were inspired by what you saw or heard.

**Notes to Myself**

_____

_____

_____

_____

Now try this: whether it was something new you learned, something that inspired you to take action, or something you applied at work, e-mail or call the presenters and let them know what you got from their presentation (even if it was four months ago). Be succinct and considerate and ask a question that will help you learn even more. If you ask a relevant and meaningful question, it's likely you'll get an equally meaningful answer. That answer will quite likely broaden and deepen your learning as well as possibly begin the start of a new professional relationship that may grow in years to come.

## Learn from Your Senior Leaders

Your interactions with senior leaders—everyone from your supervisor or your director to senior management, those heading up your association, and thought leaders in your field—can all be fantastic opportunities to understand more about the top-of-mind issues, perspectives, and big-picture thinking of those who make the decisions, set policies, and engage in the planning and direction of your field. Talking with, corresponding with, and listening to these leaders can deepen your connection to your field, and it can also be advantageous to your career. Here are some great advantages of engaging with your senior leaders:

- You'll learn more about future plans for the information organization or library location where you work (or hope to work someday).

- If you ask focused questions, you'll learn more about current or soon-to-be initiatives that you may not have heard about otherwise. Such information will give you additional ideas about the best opportunities to explore.

- You'll discover plans that may affect your branch, your department, or even your own position in the near future.

- You'll hear about concerns and thorny issues they're trying to resolve.

- You will get an important perspective on what these decision makers are thinking.

About now, you may be thinking, *Great, but how often do I get to interact with senior leaders and big thinkers in the field?* My answer: more often than you realize, if you're strategic about it.

Here are some suggestions to consider as you decide how, when, and with whom you want to initiate your interactions with senior leaders: First, consider who: the interactions that will be most useful to you—and most rewarding to both you and the person you interact with—are ones that come from a sincere desire on your part to interact with a particular person or group of leaders. This is *not* shallow networking. You and I both know that's not helpful. Consider leaders you truly want to interact with—pick three or four that you know you'd like to talk with or listen to.

Next, with your "I would like to engage with these people" list in mind, consider opportunities for reaching out. Can you ask for brief informal mentoring from some of them on specific areas? Approaches to mentoring have changed so much in recent years. Years ago, a mentoring relationship may have been a long-term (sometimes arranged) proposition that could be time-consuming for the mentor and a bit intimidating for the mentee. Current approaches are much more expansive. You don't need a formal program to be mentored. You can ask someone yourself. In fact, you can ask more than one person! When you ask for mentoring, specify a shorter time frame, what you'd like to be mentored on and why, and how you believe this person could help you. Ask how this relationship could be shaped into a workable one for your potential mentor (perhaps a once- or twice-a-week e-mail check-in, a weekly phone or Skype call, or whatever arrangement might work for that person and for you) and suggest what you could offer in return (e.g., a promise to forward articles on specific areas of interest to this person or an agreement to take notes for an upcoming conference and pass them on to your potential mentor).

Here are some other ideas to consider:

- If you have a supervisor or department leader you've gotten to know a bit already, you could offer to do a mini-research project on an area you're both interested in.

- Introduce yourself to different leaders you want to get to know at the next association meeting you both attend. Ask to be on a committee with others you know you'd love to get to know better or work with on a project.

- Volunteer to represent your department or task force at an upcoming meeting and initiate a brief conversation with leaders at that meeting who are on your list.

## Do an Informational Interview (or Do Several!)

Informational interviews have long been a valuable tool for people who are in job search mode or considering a transition to another field. But informational interviews don't have to be just for job-seekers! They can work for all professionals who are interested in growing their careers. Here's how. Let's imagine for a moment that you have become absolutely fascinated with data analysis. You enjoy the work you're doing now, but at a recent presentation you attended, you got really excited about data analysis. And you're sure that knowledge and training in data analysis could provide you with opportunities to make the services you offer now even more useful— and you're also sure that learning more in this new area could rejuvenate your passion for the field. Why not begin to learn even more about your new obsession? Of course, there are dozens of ways you could learn more. One sure way is by talking with professionals who are already doing the kind of work you've recently become interested in. Why not contact a few people (you can get names from association directories, your colleagues, nearby universities with classes on your particular topic of interest, or simply by reaching out to the person whose presentation got you excited in the first place).

Once you've made contact, ask for an informational interview (in person, if possible) and explain why you would like to talk with this person. Informational interviews are an excellent way to learn more about a topic that could represent a growth opportunity for you down the road—you can find out how to gain in-depth knowledge in the particular area, find out about the training/education it would take, learn what it would be like to use this knowledge daily in your own work, and inquire about associations or meetings that can further your learning even more

## Befriend Your IDP

You might immediately recognize the acronym IDP (Individual Development Plan) because the organization you work for uses this term. Or you may not recognize it at all—but even if you're not familiar with the acronym, I would bet that your organization uses another term to get at the same idea. Basically, an IDP is an agreement of sorts between you and your boss, usually developed during a meeting in which the two of you discuss and determine how you will further develop your career/job/role going forward over the next six months or year. IDPs are often scheduled for review annually and occasionally may come up as part of a performance review (though many organizations are separating these development discussions from performance reviews).

Many employees have come to dread the IDP discussion with their supervisor, in part because these discussions are too focused on performance and what an employee should do better; others dislike them because they see the IDP as a formality—a once-and-done type of ritual that has to be completed for the benefit of management regularly. But the IDP discussion can really become much more of an opportunity if you (and the person you are meeting with) are willing to turn your IDP mandatory meeting into a dialogue about how you'd like to grow and contribute more to your organization. (Look back at chapter 8, where we cover career conversations in more detail to get some ideas on how to make this happen.)

As writer Paula Asinof reminds us, one of the primary goals of an IDP is for leaders, managers, and supervisors to help employees "chart a career path by identifying new knowledge, skills, and abilities to pursue, as well as learning activities to reach goals."[1] And that rationale for the IDP can work in your favor! Let's assume that prior to meeting with your boss for your IDP discussion, you've taken the time to identify the best organization-focused or organization-sponsored growth opportunities for yourself. Since that will certainly be a major focus of your discussion, why not walk into your meeting with specific ideas about how you can develop yourself further and, at the same time, help your organization by contributing to its goals at the same time. If you can outline specific development activities to pursue, a timeline for completing them, and a solid rationale for how they will help you grow in your role and contribute to your organization, then you have made a compelling case! And if you have detailed your plan in a way that garners your supervisor's support, you've also made his job easier.

## Promote Yourself

*No, I'm not suggesting you need a megaphone, a website, or one thousand LinkedIn connections!*

But I am suggesting that it's in your best interests to not hide your light under a basket. Pursuing growth opportunities can be rewarding in its own right. Additionally, it is an excellent way to demonstrate your strengths, your willingness to learn new skills and knowledge, and your commitment to your career and your field. If you sincerely feel good about choosing to continue growing yourself, then why keep it a secret? By taking on growth opportunities, you set in motion a process that often leads to uncovering more opportunities—especially ones that you can get excited about. People learn about what you're doing, and many will naturally want to support your growth. But that depends on your making them aware of what you're up to. Consider these ways to do that.

### Branding

Sure, you've heard the word before—and you may have already taken steps to craft and promote your personal brand. That's great! If you've decided "branding" isn't for you (after all, you're not a high-tech worker in Silicon Valley or a marketing strategist for some online luxury service), I urge you to delve a bit more into personal branding and see how it might work for you. Consider your brand as simply the perception that others have of you, based on how you "show up" for whatever work you're doing (including your attitude, your level of professionalism, your consistency across time, and your way of presenting yourself). If you're seriously pursuing growth opportunities, my guess is that you want others to notice your commitment to your work, your high level of professionalism, and your can-do attitude.

Personal branding strategist Susan Chritton explains branding in this way: "Your personal brand is your reputation. . . . Your personal brand is also . . . the way others remember you through your actions, your expertise and the emotional connections that you make."[2]

Your brand can help you communicate who you are to others, set you apart from others in the job search, and help you build your network—the central reason to consider branding here is to help you make others aware of your work and your growth efforts.

I invite you to rethink the idea of "personal branding" without getting overwhelmed by it. Consider it a tool to share with others the particular way in which you choose to make a difference. Additionally, taking the time to promote your own brand represents the new career smarts. In the words of author Dorie Clark, "If we don't control our own narrative and show the world what we can contribute, odds are very few people will actually notice. By following these strategies [for personal branding], you dramatically increase the odds that your true talents will get known, recognized, and appreciated."[3]

## Be Known for Finishing What You Start

As you pursue the growth opportunities you've chosen, others will likely hear about it—because you shared your Growth Plan with them or because they have noticed an uptick in activities you're involved in. It's important that others *do* know what you're up to. Growing your career should *not* be a secret. Because others are aware of what you're doing, it's important that these people are also aware of your ability to finish the activities you've chosen to pursue. You can have big ideas, awesome plans, and a full calendar, but if you're known mostly for starting but not finishing, then you're demonstrating some self-defeating behaviors. And that's the opposite of what you're intending to do. *Forbes Magazine* contributor Sally Blount refers to this as "closing earlier loops before opening too many new ones." As she puts it, "You want to be known as someone who thinks strategically *and* delivers operationally. You don't want to be 'the guy/gal' with great ideas but not follow-through, and you don't want your boss wondering 'whatever happened about X . . . ?'"[4] What you do at work gets noticed, and your reputation is something you build consciously or unconsciously. So why not be known as someone who follows through?

## Time to Get Personal

We've been focusing on professional career-growth opportunities up until now. Of course, that *is* the focus of this book. Equally important, though, are growth opportunities that have little or nothing to do with work. Most of us can agree (at least, I think we can!) that the quality of our lives, overall, is more important than any one activity (even our work) that we engage in. If we're not healthy, or don't have a good mix of work/nonwork pursuits and pleasures, we're lopsided! And we'll never be able to contribute our best efforts to our work when we're out of balance regularly. Sure, we can succeed for a brief period of time. But ignoring other aspects of our lives over the long term can lead to burn out, isolation, health concerns, and diminished life satisfaction. While you may be feeling like you've heard this message a thousand times before, I want to emphasize it here in terms of the challenge an ongoing unbalanced lifestyle can represent for all of us—especially for those of us who help, support, and serve others. Though we don't intend to, we often end up last on our own list.

Here are some practices that will keep you nourished while you're pursuing the important work you're doing and also while you are putting effort into continuing to grow your career.

## Practice Amazing Self-Care

Each of us may have different criteria for self-care—but all of us know what it means, even though we may gloss over the need to do it, or we postpone it for another day when we'll have more time (which, of course, never seems to happen). For self-care to truly work, it can't be an add-on, or a special event, or something grabbed at in desperation when we realize we've pushed too hard for too long. It has to be a part of who we are. As writer Annie Dillard puts it, "How we spend our days is, of course, how we spend our lives."[5]

I once coached a library staffer who told me she couldn't stand to read this quote by Dillard because each time she saw it, it reminded her of how little she was doing to care for herself properly. Yet we can all fall into this trap of putting off our own well-being. But consider this: if you've read this far into this book, it's likely that you're serious about growing your career and demonstrating your best self to make a difference in the world. If that's the case, then you'll need a relatively healthy, solid, and positive lifestyle to make that happen. Our own self-care can't be constantly rescheduled while we take care of other things. We need to attend to it now—and tomorrow too!

## Rest

In an article he did for *The Cut*, author Brad Stulberg asked readers an interesting question: "When [was] the last time you closed Twitter feeling refreshed?" His point? Though many of the nonwork activities we engage in might *feel* restful, in fact, they may not be. He goes on to say, "Rest is so important to working in a happy, healthy, and sustainable manner that we'd be wise to think of it, not as something separate from doing good work, but rather, as an integral part of doing good work; sometimes, not working *is* the work."[6]

Take some time right now to jot down at least two activities here that fall into the category of a "restful activity." Include one you're already doing (that you intend to continue doing), but also add one or two new ones that can easily be pursued without additional cost or needing to travel somewhere else to do it (in other words, something you can incorporate into your day right now).

**📝 Notes to Myself**

_____

_____

_____

_____

## Take an Awe Walk

Words like *wonderstruck* and *awe* aren't part of our day-to-day vocabulary. Such words may remind us of an experience from our childhood, but we don't usually associate them with our daily experiences as adults. Yet the power of experiencing a sense of awe or wonder can't be underestimated, and we shouldn't dismiss opportunities to reconnect with such feelings. Juliana Breines, writing for the *Huffington Post*, reintroduces us to these words. Citing the work done by the Greater Good Science Center and research from the University of California, Berkeley, Breines explains *awe* this way: "Researchers define awe as the feeling we get in the presence of something larger than ourselves that challenges our usual way of seeing the world. A great work of art, a breathtaking vista, a moving speech, the first flowers of spring—these can all evoke awe."[7]

We already recognize the restorative power of spending time in nature, untethered from our electronic devices and the noisy human-made sounds that surround us. A walk in the woods, a few minutes spent kicking off our shoes and socks to feel the grass beneath our feet, can reconnect us with the essentials. Now new research is suggesting that experiencing awe can have therapeutic and health benefits and help both children and adults thrive.

As an excellent self-care practice, these walks, even short ones, can offer a simple way to nurture yourself. If you are up for trying one, Breines has some suggestions:

> One way to create more opportunities for awe is to approach your surroundings with fresh eyes, as if you're seeing them for the first time. Otherwise ordinary features—a bird singing, the color of the sky—may be transformed into something

more extraordinary. But it's also possible to integrate an Awe Walk into your daily routine—even if a route is familiar to you, you can make an effort to notice new things. The same old sights you pass every day may turn out to be surprising sources of inspiration.[8]

## Hone the Art of Resilience

We may not automatically think of resilience as a career development tool, but it definitely is. In addition to a proven way to boost our self-care score and nurture our physical and mental well-being, the practice of resilience keeps us career-ready by keeping us adaptable and flexible—able to meet whatever workplace challenges come our way.

It's all about the bounce, really. That's often how people describe resilience—as their ability to bounce back from the stresses they encounter in their daily lives.

Before we go any further, why not rate your own resilience? Here's a quick question for you:

 **Notes to Myself**

**Just how resilient are you? Check the statement that reflects how you feel most of the time:**

_____ I bounce back from challenges most of the time.

_____ I am finding it harder to bounce back from challenges lately.

_____ I've lost my "bounce."

• • •

So how did you do? Wherever you are on the resilience spectrum right now, there are some things you can do to safeguard your resilience reserves. The first action you can take is to become more aware of when you're starting to feel depleted.

In addition to becoming more aware of factors that may deplete your resilience, there are a number of actions you can take to enhance your resilience reserves.

- Rediscover your sense of wholeheartedness—recall those moments and activities when you truly felt you were 100 percent engaged— whether it was a specific project or activity, or a particular group of colleagues you spent time with. See if you can build more "wholeheart-ed" moments back into your day.

- Establish "no multitasking" zones at work and at home. Put up a sign if you need to, something like "No multitasking allowed here!" Such reminders can help you focus again, without distraction. You'll find several books, tapes, and articles on practices to help you focus—and guess where you can access them? Yep . . . your local library!

- Keep reminders near where you spend much of your workday and at home too that can reinforce a sense of calm—perhaps favorite pictures, mementos from special places or events, soothing music, items from the natural world—anything that makes you smile or pause and breathe deeply.

## Practice Mindfulness at Work (and Just About Anywhere Else Too!)

You've probably seen the word *mindfulness* everywhere lately. I know I have. There's mindful eating, mindful walking, mindful parenting, and mindfulness in challeng-ing conversations. The list goes on. But don't dismiss mindfulness as just another buzzword or fad. Quite likely, one of the reasons mindfulness has been showing up so often in so many different places—from corporate leadership programs to well-ness offerings—is that it presents a compelling case for an alternate response to our lightning-paced and increasingly complex workplace that comes with so many de-mands and expectations. Mindfulness requires that we slow down, reflect, and act out of increased awareness. It's one of those ideas that sounds simple but isn't necessar-ily easy. Research on mindfulness shows that it is an ancient practice, often coupled with meditation, that focuses on moment-to-moment awareness—both of our world around us and what's happening there as well as what's going on inside of us, includ-ing our thoughts and feelings. The intent of mindfulness is to get us off autopilot and onto a fully present consciousness so that we act in mindful, purposeful ways—what-ever it is that we're doing.

Consider mindfulness a regular part of your daily routine as a way to take better care of yourself. If you do, chances are high that you'll relieve some stress and anxiety, reap some additional physical benefits, and find yourself more centered as you go about your work.

One last suggestion on your mindfulness practice: take it home with you when your workday ends too!

# Growth Doesn't Just Happen at Work

While we generally think of professional growth as happening mostly at work, it's important to recognize that significant growth can happen through nonwork-related activities too. Activities don't always need to have a work connection for them to add value to one's career. When we acknowledge that we all bring our "whole selves" to work with us each day, it's easier to see how any activity—or action we take—has the possibility of enhancing our growth. One library support person I talked with put it this way: "It's not like I leave 20 percent of myself in my car in the parking lot when I come into work each day. I bring in all of me!" With that in mind, it makes sense that what we do in our away-from-work hours can also contribute to the quality of our work and the value we offer our employers and those we serve and support.

To give you a better idea of what I mean, take a look at the activities of these different professionals. Claude, a collections development librarian, volunteers four times a year at Habitat for Humanity. Susan, a knowledge management professional, returns to the same city in Guatemala each year to assist local health care workers at a regional health clinic. And Cassie, a public library staffer, teaches literacy skills twice a week to refugees in her hometown.

What these three professionals have in common is a desire to help and be of service to others. And in the process of pursuing these opportunities, you can bet that they learn a lot about compassion, servant leadership, and understanding the needs of others. Clearly, they carry their experiences and the lessons they've learned back with them when they return to their workplaces, where they continue to make a difference.

While these three examples represent volunteer activities, there are dozens of other possibilities to grow from nonwork-related activities. Here is an example: Imagine you've always wanted to learn other languages. Your fascination with other languages and cultures may prompt you to enroll in language courses and travel to locations where you can practice your newly acquired language skills. These activities might ignite a dream to live and work in another part of the world.

Reflect for a few minutes here on passions or dreams you may have set aside or activities that have been on your bucket list for far too long. Is there one (or more) that would be possible to pursue now? After you've reflected on this a bit, respond to the questions on the next page.

## Notes to Myself

**What is it that you're interested in doing?**

_____

_____

_____

**Why does this activity hold so much interest or curiosity for you?**

_____

_____

_____

**How do you think pursuing this activity might affect or change you? (Even a short vacation to a favorite spot can ease stress, increase your chance to play a bit, and recharge your batteries!)**

_____

_____

_____

## You Don't Have to Do _More_!

Remember, growth does not necessarily mean always doing _more_ of something, just like advancement doesn't necessarily mean needing to take a promotion or move to the next step up the organizational ladder.

Opportunities for growth (both work-related and nonwork-related) can mean doing less. Perhaps it can mean saying no to an additional request that's not part of your role—if that gives you more of an opportunity to focus on a challenging task in front of you. Or it may mean saying no to a new opportunity—if it means you'll have more time to spend with family or friends (and that's a top priority in your life right now). Less may mean rebalancing your work schedule, choosing a smaller role in a committee that you're a part of, or choosing to cut back on responsibilities in some other part of your life. At times, growth can be happening internally (e.g., focusing on becoming more compassionate, more reflective, or more able to see a broader view of what's happening around you); this growth may not be easily observable to anyone else (only to you). You're the one who decides which type of growth opportunities are the best ones for you at any given time.

## It Does Take a Village

It's true—early in this book, I talked about the new "career model" being one best described as YoYo ("You're on Your own"). And while it's likely that the organization you work for is expecting you to be in charge of your own career progress, that philosophy doesn't mean you are totally alone, isolated, and without support. As formal, organization-sponsored responsibility for your career fades, newer types of support, encouragement, and models to sustain your career growth efforts are emerging.

Inside your organization or association, there are multiple sources of support from mentorship and sponsorship to ALA's Emerging Leaders Program (as well as several other committees and roundtable discussion groups).

At the individual level, it's always an option to connect with a colleague or two and set up an informal way of meeting to discuss your career aspirations and goals and get support from one another. Several years ago, author Barbara Sher, a career consultant, developed the idea of success teams (mentioned earlier in chapter 7).[9] The intent of the team is to people to form a group (composed of friends, colleagues, spouses, or partners) with the commitment to get together regularly and report to the group on one's successes as well as ask for feedback, advice, and support in moving forward toward one's goals. (I recall being a member of one of these groups and still have wonderful memories of being able to both get support and celebrate one another's successes.) You may want to put together such a group yourself.

**Imagine starting this type of group now—who would you include? Why? How could you make it workable (don't forget that Skype and other online platforms might help)?**

_____

_____

_____

_____

Don't forget the support of family as well. Family here refers to your spouse, partner, children, and parents—and it also includes a definition of *family* that is represented by a circle of close friends who cherish and encourage you. Often, when we share our dreams of what we aspire to, we get more encouragement than we ever imagined.

The bottom line here? Don't try to go it alone. You don't need to. Find and accept support in ways that work for you—don't be shy about asking for what you need and don't forget to reciprocate—that's the real definition of *support*.

## What's *Your* Touchstone?

It's important to have reminders of special occasions and peaceful moments to keep us in a calm and composed space. It's even *more* important to have a personal touchstone that keeps us focused, centered, clear about our purpose and goals, and mindful of our competence and confidence as we go about the many aspects of our professional lives.

Touchstones can be pictures, quotes, or a section of a book or audiotape that has significant meaning for you. Likewise, it can be a memory of an important event or person in your life that you can access anytime you need to by finding a quiet corner, closing your eyes, and taking a few minutes to bring this image to mind. Whatever form it takes, your personal touchstone should help remind you of what matters most to you, your vision of your very best self, or your vision for your future—contributing your best talents to make the difference you truly want to make. I encourage you to be thoughtful about choosing your touchstone, take the time to choose one that truly resonates with you, and keep it close to help you see all the potential opportunities that are open to you.

## ✎ Notes to Myself

**Spend some quiet time reflecting on what form your own touchstone might take. Note your ideas here.**

_____

_____

_____

Make a commitment to yourself to make this touchstone a part of your life, starting now!

## Notes

1. Paula Asinof, "IDPs: Development's Superglue," *T & D Magazine*, January 20, 2016, www.td.org/magazines/td-magazine/idps-talent-developments-superglue/.
2. Susan Chritton, "Personal Branding and You," *Huffington Post*, April 22, 2013, www.huffingtonpost.com/susan-chritton/personal-brands_b_2729249.html.
3. Dorie Clark, "How Women Can Develop—and Promote—Their Personal Brand," *Harvard Business Review*, March 2, 2018, https://hbr.org/2018/03/how-women-can-develop-and-promote-their-personal-brand/.
4. Sally Blount, "Six Ways to Demonstrate You're Promotion-Ready," *Forbes*, September 1, 2017, www.forbes.com/sites/sallyblount/2017/09/01/six-ways-to-demonstrate-youre-promotion-ready/#3f36d8a91202/.
5. BrainyQuote.com, "Annie Dillard Quotes," www.brainyquote.com/authors/annie_dillard/.
6. Brad Stulberg, "How to Actually Get Some Rest for Once," *The Cut*, October 4, 2017, www.thecut.com/2017/10/how-to-actually-get-some-rest-for-once.html.
7. Juliana Breines, "4 Awe-Inspiring Activities," *Huffington Post*, December 6, 2017, https://huffingtonpost.com/greater-good-science-center/four/awe/inspiring/activities_b_9433494.html.
8. Ibid.
9. Barbara Sher with Annie Gottlieb, *Wishcraft: How to Get What You Really Want* (New York: Ballantine Books, 2004).

# My *Going for It!* Growth Plan

Congratulations! You've already taken a *huge* step forward by reading through this book, reflecting on the ideas presented here, and completing the exercises within it. Clearly, you're committed to your own professional growth. This last section, "My *Going for It!* Growth Plan," gives you the opportunity (isn't *opportunity* a wonderful word?) to put all that reflection into action. Beginning on the next page, you'll see your own personal *Going for It!* Growth Plan. You already began to fill this plan in when you completed the assignment listed near the end of chapter 8. Now you can fill in the remaining sections of your plan! I urge you to do so now while your thoughts, ideas, and excitement about your own growth are fresh in your mind.

Consider this plan, once you've filled in all of it, to be your personally designed path to shaping your career in just the way you want to. As you finish your first round of choosing, pursuing, and completing your growth opportunities and you've had the time to fully appreciate all you've learned from them, set your sights on continuing to grow. You will find a template of this plan online at alaeditions.org/webextras. Make as many copies you want to so that you can use this same "formula" for growing your career over and over again.

I wish you every possible success as you go forward on your career growth adventures!

# My *Going for It!* Growth Plan

**Section 1: This is how I would like to grow right now!**

_____

_____

_____

**Section 2: The top growth opportunities that will get me moving in that direction are:**

*Longer-term Opportunities*                    *Shorter-term Opportunities*

_____          _____

_____          _____

_____          _____

**My timeline for beginning and completing these opportunities that I have listed above:**

*Longer-term Opportunities*                    *Shorter-term Opportunities*

# My *Going for It!* Growth Plan (page 2)

**Section 3: My opportunity tracker**

*Before* **I begin:**

**I'm going to pursue this opportunity:**

_____

**because:**

_____

*While* **I am pursuing the opportunity:**

**What I'm learning so far is:**

_____

**The ups include:**

_____

**The downs include:**

_____

**What I didn't expect:**

_____

**What I'm learning about myself:**

_____

# My *Going for It!* Growth Plan (page 3)

*After* I have completed the opportunity:

What I learned through this opportunity:

_____

What I learned about myself:

_____

What I'm going to do with this knowledge, skill, or new way of going about my work:

_____

When?

_____

How does this knowledge fit (or not fit) with the way I want to grow?

_____

# My *Going for It!* Growth Plan (page 4)

**Section 4: What's next for me?**

**Take on a new opportunity (which one)?**

_____

**Take a new direction?**

_____

**Are there any decisions I need to make now?**

_____

**Is there anyone I need to talk with because of my new learning from the opportunity I just completed?**

_____

**Is there anything I want to do differently?**

_____

**How am I different since completing my last opportunity (new perspective, new skills, new behaviors, etc.)? In other words, what (if anything) has changed?**

_____

My *Going for It!* Growth Plan is available online from alaeditions.org/webextras.

# Bibliography

Acevedo, Tamara. "The Accidental Librarian." In *Making the Most of Your Library Career*, edited by Lois Stickell and Bridgette Sanders, 21–30. Chicago: American Library Association, 2014.

Acuff, Jon. *Do Over: Make Today the First Day of Your New Career*. New York: Penguin, 2017.

ALISE Association for Library and Information Science Education. "Guidelines for Practices and Principles in the Design, Operation, and Evaluation of Post-master's Residency Programs." *Library Personnel News* 10, no. 3 (1996): 1–3.

Allard, Suzie. "Placements & Salaries 2017: Librarians Everywhere." *Library Journal*, October 17, 2017. https://lj.libraryjournal.com/2017/10/placements-and-salaries/2017-survey/librarians-everywhere/#_/.

American Library Association. "ALA Emerging Leaders Program." www.ala.org/education careers/leadership/emergingleaders/.

———. "ALA Job List." https://joblist.ala.org/.

———. "Trends." Center for the Future of Libraries. www.ala.org/tools/future/trends/.

Asinof, Paula. "IDPs: Development's Superglue." *T & D Magazine*, January 20, 2016. www.td.org/magazines/td-magazine/idps-talent-developments-superglue/.

Azulay, Halelly. *Employee Development on a Shoestring*. Alexandria, VA: ASTD Press, 2012.

Bakhshi, Hasan, Jonathan Downing, Michael Osborne, and Philippe Schneider. "The Top 10 Occupations Predicted to Experience Increased Demand through 2030." In *Future of Skills: Employment in 2030*. London: Pearson and Nesta, 2017. www.nesta.org.uk/sites/default/files/the_future_of_skills_employment_in_2030_0.pdf.

Barron, Allyce. "Professional Development, One Bite at a Time." *Training & Development*, March 2014, 70–73.

Bennett, Nathan, and G. James Lemoine. "What VUCA Really Means for You." *Harvard Business Review*, January–February 2014. http://hbr.org/2014/01/what-vuca-really-means-for-you/ar/pr/.

Blount, Sally. "Six Ways to Demonstrate You're Promotion-Ready." *Forbes*, September 1, 2017. www.forbes.com/sites/sallyblount/2017/09/01/six-ways-to-demonstrate-youre-promotion-ready/#3f36d8a91202/.

Bohnet, Iris. "Tackling 'The Thin File' That Can Prevent a Promotion." *New York Times*, October 3, 2017. www.nytimes.com/2017/10/03/business/women-minority-promotion.html.

BrainyQuote.com. "Annie Dillard Quotes." www.brainyquote.com/authors/annie_dillard/.

Breines, Juliana. "4 Awe-Inspiring Activities." *Huffington Post*, December 6, 2017. https://huffingtonpost.com/greater-good-science-center/four/awe/inspiring/activities_b_9433494.html.

Bridges, William. *JobShift: How to Prosper in a Workplace without Jobs*. New York: Perseus Books, 1994.

BusinessDictionary.com. "Backcasting." www.businessdictionary.com/definition/backcasting.html.

Byrd, Bretagne. Phone interview with the author. November 2, 2017.

Calvin, Beatrice. Phone interview with the author. January 19, 2018.

Cartoonstock.com. "Libraries." www.cartoonstock.com/sitesearch.asp?categories=All+Categories&artists=All+Artists&mainArchive=mainArchive&newsCartoon=newsCartoon&vintage=vintage&ANDkeyword=libraries&searchBoxButton=SEARCH/.

Carucci, Ron. "Why Everyone Needs a Portfolio Career." *Forbes*, September 25, 2017. www.forbes.com/sites/roncarucci/2017/09/25/three-reasons-everyone-needs-a-portfolio-career/#59ec4b5e4d07/.

Cascio, Jamais. "Futures Thinking: Mapping the Possibilities, Part 2." *Fast Company*, February 12, 2010. www.fastcompany.com/1547923/futures/thinking-mapping-possibilities-part-2/.

Chritton, Susan. "Personal Branding and You." *Huffington Post*, April 22, 2013. www.huffingtonpost.com/susan-chritton/personal-brands_b_2729249.html.

Clark, Dorie. "How Women Can Develop—and Promote—Their Personal Brand." *Harvard Business Review*, March 2, 2018. https://hbr.org/2018/03/how-women-can-develop-and-promote-their-personal-brand/.

Clear, James. "Core-Value List." https://jamesclear.com/core-values/.

Davey, Liane. "You Can Learn and Get Work Done at the Same Time." *Harvard Business Review*, January 11, 2016. https://hbr.org/2016/01/you-can-learn-and-get-work-done-at-the-same-time/.

Dictionary.com. "Attitude." www.dictionary.com/browse/attitude?s=t/.

———. "Mind-set." www.dictionary.com/browse/mindset?s=t/.

———. "Opportunity." www.dictionary.com/browse/opportunity?s=t.

Dority, G. Kim. *Rethinking Information Work: A Career Guide for Librarians and Other Information Professionals*. 2nd ed. Santa Barbara, CA: Libraries Unlimited, 2016.

Doyle, Alison. "What Are Soft Skills?" *The Balance*, April 14, 2018. www.thebalance.com/what-are-soft-skills-2060852/.

———. "What Are the Hard Skills Employers Seek?" *The Balance*, April 17, 2018. www.thebalance.com/what-are-hard-skills-2060829/.

Doyle, Patrick, Mitch Gelman, and Sam Gill. "Viewing the Future? Virtual Reality in Storytelling." Knight Foundation, March 13, 2016. www.knightfoundation.org/reports/vrjournalism/.

Draudt, Alida, and Julia Rose West. *What the Foresight: Your Personal Futures Explored. Defy the Expected and Define the Preferred*. Self-published, CreateSpace, April 27, 2016.

Drucker, Peter. "Managing Oneself." *Harvard Business Review*, January 2005.

Dweck, Carol S. *Mindset: The New Psychology of Success*. New York: Ballantine Books, 2006.

Farber, Steve. "Six Critical Steps You Must Take Before Every Big Decision." *Inc.*, March 9, 2018. www.inc.com/steve-farber/6-critical-steps-you-must-take-before-every-big-decision.html.

Farnam Street. "The Difference between Amateurs and Professionals." n.d. www.fs.blog/2017/08/amateurs-professionals/.

Financial Times. "Pivot." http://lexicon.ft.com/Term?term=pivot/.

Goia, Joyce. "Employability in the New World of Work." *Herman Trend Alert*, July 12, 2017. www.hermangroup.com/alert/archive_7-12-2017.html.

Godin, Seth. *The Dip: A Little Book That Teaches You When to Quit (and When to Stick)*. New York: Penguin Group, 2007.

———. *Linchpin: Are You Indispensable?* New York: Penguin Group, 2010.

———. *Poke the Box: When Was the Last Time You Did Something for the First Time?* New York: Portfolio, 2015.

Goldsmith, Marshall. *What Got You Here Won't Get You There*. New York: Hyperion Books, 2007.

Hansen, Katharine. "Job Shadowing: An Overview." www.experience.com/advice/job-search/networking/job-shadowing-an-overview/.

Harkness, Helen. "The YoYo Model for Your Future Career: You're On Your Own." *Career Planning and Adult Development Journal* 24, no. 2 (Summer 2008): 10.

Huang, Hannah. Phone interview with the author. November 2017.

Immelt, Jeffrey R. "How I Remade GE and What I Learned along the Way." *Harvard Business Review*, August 24, 2017. www.alumni.hbs.edu/stories/Pages/story-bulletin.aspx?num=6377/.

Inayatullah, Sohail. "Library Futures." *The Futurist*, November–December 2014.

Institute for Policy Studies. "Income Inequality." http://inequality.org/income-inequality/.

Ito, Mimi. "Connected Learning: An Agenda for Social Change," *Huffington Post*, January 15, 2013. www.huffingtonpost.com/mimi-ito/connected-learning_b_2478940.html.

Jarratt, Jennifer. Personal communication with the author. 2000.

Jett, Charles Cranston. *The DOOM LOOP! Straight Talk about Job Frustration, Boredom, Career Crises and Tactical Career Decisions from the Doom Loop Creator*. Denver, CO: Outskirts Press, 2015.

The Job Analysis and Information Section Division of Standards and Research. *Dictionary of Occupational Titles*. Part 1, *Definitions of Titles*. Washington, DC: US Government Printing Office, 1939.

Kahn, Herman. "The Expert and Educated Incapacity." Hudson Institute, June 1, 1979. www.hudson.org/research/2219-the-expert-and-educated-incapacity/.

Kaye, Beverly L. *A Guide to Career Development Practitioners: Up Is Not the Only Way*. San Diego: University Associates, 1985.

Kaye, Beverly, Lindy Williams, and Lynn Cowart. *Up Is Not the Only Way: Rethinking Career Mobility*. San Francisco: Berrett-Koehler, 2017.

Kaye, Beverly, and Julie Giulioni. *Help Them Grow or Watch Them Go: Career Conversations Employees Want*. San Francisco: Berrett-Koehler, 2012.

Koba, Mark. "Returnships for Older Workers: Proceed with Caution." *CNBC*, October 15, 2013. www.cnbc.com/2013/10/14/returnships-for-older-workers-proceed-with-caution.html.

Kokemuller, Neil. "How to Demonstrate Adaptability on the Job." Chron. http://work.chron.com/demonstrate-adaptability-job-15407.html.

Kuehner-Hebert, Katie. "Career Advice Key to Post-growth Development." *Chief Learning Officer*, November 4, 2014. www.clomedia.com/2014/11/04/career-advice-key-to-post growth-development/.

Leslie, Ian. *Curious: The Desire to Know and Why Your Future Depends on It*. Philadelphia: Basic Books, 2014.

Levoy, Gregg Michael. *Finding and Following an Authentic Life*. New York: Crown, 1998.

Lum, Richard A. K. *4 Steps to the Future: A Quick and Clean Guide to Creating Foresight*. Honolulu, HI: Vision Foresight Strategy, 2016.

Markel, Adam. *Pivot: The Art and Science of Reinventing Your Career and Life*. New York: Atria, 2016.

Maxey, Lee. "Bridging the Last Mile." *Chief Learning Officer*, August 11, 2017. www.clomedia .com/2017/08/11/bridging-last-mile-close-skills-gap/.

McKee, Annie. "Happiness Traps." *Harvard Business Review*, September–October 2017. https://hbr.org/2017/09/happiness-traps/.

Mediavilla, Cynthia. "Conducting a Yearlong Fellowship Program." In *Continuing Education for Librarians*, edited by Carol Smallwood, Kerol Harrod, and Vera Gubnitskaia, 79–87. Jefferson, NC: McFarland, 2013.

Merriam-Webster. "Über-." www.merriam-webster.com/dictionary/über-/.

MindTools.com. "What Are Your Values?" www.mindtools.com/pages/article/newTED_ 85.htm.

Moran, Gwen. "How to Help Build Employees' Career Paths So They Don't Quit." *American Psychological Association's Center for Organizational Excellence*, November 3, 2017. www .fastcompany.com/40490723/how-to-help-build-employees-career-paths-so-they-dont -quit/.

Mozilla Foundation and Peer 2 Peer University, in collaboration with the MacArthur Foun- dation. "Open Badges for Lifelong Learning: Exploring an Open Badge Ecosystem to Support Skill Development and Lifelong Learning for Real Results Such as Jobs and Advancement." January 23, 2013. https://wiki.mozilla.org/images/b/b1/OpenBadges -Working-Paper_092011.pdf.

MyWorldofWork.com. "What Are My Strengths?" www.myworldofwork.co.uk/my-career -options/what-are-my-strengths/.

Obama, Barack. "Remarks by the President on Economic Mobility." The White House, De- cember 4, 2013. www.whitehouse.gov/the-press-office/2013/12/04/remarks-president-/.

Oden, Michael. "Best of Both Worlds: The Advantages of a Dual-Library Internship." *Ameri- can Libraries Magazine*, January–February 2017.

Oremus, Will. "Terrifyingly Convenient." *Slate*, April 3, 2016. www.slate.com/articles/technology/ cover_story/2016/04/alexa_corta/.

Oxford Dictionary. "Adaptable." https://en.oxforddictionaries.com/definition/adaptable/.

———. "Professional Development." https://en.oxforddictionaries.com/definition/professional_ development/.

———. "Savvy." https://en.oxforddictionaries.com/definition/savvy/.

———. "Uber." https://en.oxforddictionaries.com/definition/uber-.

Palmer, Erin. "Guest Post: The Importance of Self-Assessments." Benoit Central, May 17, 2012. http://benoitconsulting.com/guest-post-the-importance-of-self-assessments/.

Pandey, Asha. "5 Killer Examples: How to Use Microlearning-Based Training Effectively." eLearning Industry, April 11, 2016. https://elearningindustry.com/5-killer-examples -use-microlearning-based-training-effectively/.

Pew Research Center. "The State of American Jobs." Social and Demographic Trends, October 6, 2016, www.pewsocialtrends.org/2016/10/06/the-state-of-american-jobs/.

Prather, Hugh. *Notes to Myself.* Moab, UT: Real People Press, 1972.

Power, Sally J. *The Mid-Career Success Guide.* Westport, CT: Praeger, 2006.

Rath, Tom. *StrengthsFinder 2.0.* Omaha, NE: Gallup Press, 2007.

Reh, F. John. "Understanding Knowledge, Skills and Abilities: KSA." *The Balance,* September 10, 2017. www.thebalance.com/understanding-knowledge-skills-and-abilities -ksa-275329/.

Reilly, Jillian. "#1 Most Under-Rated Leadership Skill: Are You Curious?" Braveshift, September 26, 2017. https://braveshift.com/are-you-curious/.

Row, Heath. "Coping-Martin Seligman." *Fast Company Magazine,* November 30, 1998. www .fastcompany.com/35969/coping-martin-seligman/.

San Jose State University. "School of Information." Core Courses and Electives. http:// ischool.sjsu.edu/current-students/courses/core-courses-and-electives.

San Jose State University School of Information. "MLIS Skills at Work: A Snapshot of Job Postings." *Annual Report,* 2018. http://ischool.sjsu.edu/sites/default/files/content_ pdf/career_trends.pdf.

Schwabel, Dan. "10 Workplace Trends You'll See in 2018." *Forbes,* November 1, 2017. www .forbes.com/sites/danschawbel/2017/11/01/10-workplace-trends-youll-see-in-2018/ #1da3bfb84bf2/.

Sher, Barbara, and Annie Gottlieb. *Teamworks!* New York: Grand Central Publishing, 1991.
———. *Wishcraft: How to Get What You Really Want.* New York: Ballantine Books, 2004.

SkillsYouNeed.com. "What is Coaching?" www.skillsyouneed.com/learn/coaching.html.

Szpunar, Karl K., and Kathleen B. McDermott. "Remembering the Past to Imagine the Future." *Cerebrum,* February 15, 2007. www.dana.org/Cerebrum/Default.aspx?id=39378/.

Stulberg, Brad. "How to Actually Get Some Rest for Once." *The Cut,* October 4, 2017. www .thecut.com/2017/10/how-to-actually get-some-rest-for-once.html.

Tirard, Antoine, and Claire-Harbour-Lyell. "The Mindset That Fosters Agility." INSEAD. https://knowledge.insead.edu/blog/insead-blog/the-mindset-that-fosters-career -agility-6891.

United States Department of Labor. "Librarians" in "Job Outlook." *Occupational Outlook Handbook,* last modified July 2, 2018. www.bls.gov/ooh/education-training-and-library/ librarians.htm#tab-6/.
———. "O*NET OnLine." www.onetonline.org/.
———. "What Are Values?" www.careeronestop.org/ExploreCareers/Assessments/ work-values.aspx.

Valcour, Monique. "4 Ways to Be a Better Learner." *Harvard Business Review.* www.hbrascend .in/topics/4-ways-to-become-a-better-learner/.

Vock, Daniel C. "Facing Climate Change, Cities Embrace Resiliency." *Governing,* September 2014. www.governing.com/topics/transportation-infrastructure/gov-climate -change-cities-resiliency.html.

WebJunction.com. "Audiovisual Librarians Job Descriptions." Last modified March 21, 2012. www.webjunction.org/documents/webjunction/Audiovisual_Librarian_Job_Descriptions.html.

Weeks, Aidy. Phone interview with the author. December 2017.

Weiner, Edith, and Arnold Brown. *Insider's Guide to the Future.* Greenwich, CT: Boardroom Classics, 1997.

Whitmore, John. *Coaching for Performance: The Principles and Practice of Coaching and Leadership.* Boston: Nicholas Brealey, 2017.

Wikipedia.org. "Allen Saunders." https://en.wikipedia.org/wiki/Allen_Saunders/.

———. "Backcasting." https://en.wikipedia.org/wiki/Backcasting/.

———. "Bouldering." https://en.wikipedia.org/wiki/Bouldering/.

———. "Personal Development." https://en.wikipedia.org/wiki/Personal_development/.

———. "Volatility, Uncertainty, Complexity and Ambiguity." https://en.wikipedia.org/wiki/Volatility,_uncertainty,_complexity_and_ambiguity/.

Williams, Caitlin. "The End of the Job as We Know It." *Training & Development Magazine,* January 1999.

———. *Successful Woman's Guide to Working Smart: 10 Strengths that Matter Most.* Palo Alto, CA: Davies-Black, 2001.

Young Adult Library Services Association (YALSA). "Current YALSA Task Forces." www.ala.org/yalsa/workingwithyalsa/tf/.

Zeilinger, Julie. "7 Reasons Why Risk-Taking Leads to Success." *Huffington Post,* September 25, 2017. www.huffingtonpost.com/2013/08/13/seven-reasons-why-risk-taking-leads-to-success_n_3749425.html.

Zubernis, Lynn. "The Geek Grandpa: Leonard Nimoy's Pivotal Role in the Rise of Fandom." Raw Story, March 5, 2015. www.rawstory.com/2015/03/the-geek-grandpa-leonard-nimoys-pivotal-role-in-the-rise-of-fandom.

# Index

haptic technology as trend in libraries and librarianship, 85
Harbour-Lyell, Claire, 44
hard skills, 56–58
Harkness, Helen, 12
*Harvard Business Review,* 42
*Help Them Grow or Watch Them Go* (Kaye and Giulioni), 39
*Herman Trend Alert,* 7
"How to Help Build Employees' Career Paths So They Don't Quit" (Moran), 151
Huang, Hannah, 21

**I**

ideal work setting, imagining your, 91
identifying best opportunities, 110–112
IDPs (Individual Development Plans), 172–173
imagination and reaching your preferred future, 75
Immelt, Jeff, 31
income inequality as trend in libraries and librarianship, 86
informational interviews, 124, 171–172
initiative, need for, 43
interactions and opportunities
    IDPs (Individual Development Plans), 172–173
    informational interviews, 171–172
    mentoring, 170–171
    overview, 167–169
    presentations, 169
    senior leaders, learning from your, 170–171
Internet of Things (IoT) as trend in libraries and librarianship, 86
internships, 124–125, 133

**J**

JamesClear (website), 62
jargon in the workplace, 9–10
Jarratt, Jennifer, 55
Jett, Charles, 35, 37
job enrichment, 125
job rotation, 125
job shadowing, 128
jobs
    careers compared, 17
    descriptions of jobs from 1939 and 2012 compared, 24–25
    titles in demand, list of job, 14–15
*JobShift: How to Prosper in a Workplace without Jobs* (Bridges), 4

**K**

Kahn, Herman, 35
Kaye, Beverly, 1, 19, 39
knowledge
    defined, 50
    example of, 50–51
    gaps in your knowledge or skill set, 152–153
    Ian Leslie's view of, 52–53
    know-how and, 54
    new knowledge, opportunity to acquire, 113–114
    self-assessment of your, 51–52

T-shaped knowledge, 52–53
of yourself, need for deep, 39–40
Koba, Mark, 127
Kraft, Don, 19
KSAs (Knowledge, Skills, and Abilities)
    abilities
        attitude and, 60–61
        defined, 51
        example of, 51
        overview, 59
        self-assessment of your, 60
    knowledge
        defined, 50
        example of, 50–51
        gaps in your knowledge or skill set, 152–153
        Ian Leslie's view of, 52–53
        know-how and, 54
        new knowledge, opportunity to acquire, 113–114
        self-assessment of your, 51–52
        T-shaped knowledge, 52–53
        of yourself, need for deep, 39–40
    skills
        burnout skills, 58
        defined, 51
        in demand, list of, 15–16
        example of, 51
        gaps in your knowledge or skill set, 152–153
        hard skills, 56–58
        opportunity to acquire new, 113–114
        overview, 55
        self-assessment of your hard, 56–57
        self-assessment of your soft, 55
        soft skills, 55
        specialized skills in demand, list of, 15–16
        strengths and, 58–59
Kuehner-Hebert, Katie, 19

**L**

leadership roles, 126
leaning towards an opportunity, 113
learning
    appetite for learning, need for insatiable, 42–43
    best methods for you to learn, 152
    chunking, 153
    classes, 134
    continuing education, 123
    exciting, making learning, 152
    flipped learning as trend in libraries and librarianship, 85
    gaps in your knowledge or skill set, 152–153
    lifelong learning as trend in career and the workplace, 90
    lunch and learns, 126
    OTJ (On the Job) learning, 153
    self-directed learning, 134–135
    senior leaders, learning from your, 170–171
    and turning opportunities into realities, 151–152
learning opportunities. *See* opportunities for career-growth
Lennon, John, 64
Leslie, Ian, 52

JUL - - 2019